The Source of All Love

Catholicity in an Evolving Universe
Ilia Delio, General Editor

This series of original works by leading Catholic figures explores all facets of life through the lens of catholicity: a sense of dynamic wholeness and a conscious awareness of a continually unfolding creation.

Making All Things New: Catholicity, Cosmology, Consciousness
Ilia Delio

A New Heaven, A New Earth: The Bible and Catholicity
Dianne Bergant

CATHOLICITY IN AN EVOLVING UNIVERSE

The Source of All Love

Catholicity and the Trinity

HEIDI RUSSELL

ORBIS BOOKS
Maryknoll, New York 10545

ORBIS BOOKS
Maryknoll, New York 10545

Fathers and Brothers MARYKNOLL™

Founded in 1970, Orbis Books endeavors to publish works that enlighten the mind, nourish the spirit, and challenge the conscience. The publishing arm of the Maryknoll Fathers and Brothers, Orbis seeks to explore the global dimensions of the Christian faith and mission, to invite dialogue with diverse cultures and religious traditions, and to serve the cause of reconciliation and peace. The books published reflect the views of their authors and do not represent the official position of the Maryknoll Society. To learn more about Maryknoll and Orbis Books, please visit our website at www.maryknollsociety.org.

Published by Orbis Books, Box 302, Maryknoll, NY 10545-0302.

Portions of Chapter 2 and Chapter 6 are adapted from "From Being to Love: Reconceiving the Trinity in Light of Jean Luc Marion's Phenomenological Shift," *Horizons* 41 (2014): 22–48.

Manufactured in the United States of America.
Manuscript editing and typesetting by Joan Weber Laflamme.

Library of Congress Cataloging-in-Publication Data

Names: Russell, Heidi, 1973– author.
Title: The source of all love : Catholicity and the Trinity / Heidi Russell ; foreword by Ilia Delio.
Description: Maryknoll : Orbis Books, 2017. | Includes bibliographical references and index.
Identifiers: LCCN 2016032237 (print) | LCCN 2016036919 (ebook) | ISBN 9781626982345 (pbk.) | ISBN 9781608336982 (ebook)
Subjects: LCSH: Trinity. | Catholic Church—Doctrines. | Bohm, David, 1917–1992. | Rahner, Karl, 1904–1984. | Smolin, Lee, 1955–
Classification: LCC BT111.3 .R86 2017 (print) | LCC BT111.3 (ebook) | DDC 231/.044—dc23
LC record available at https://lccn.loc.gov/2016032237

For DJ and Ella, who ground me in love

Contents

Acknowledgments

First and foremost, I would like to thank Ilia Delio for inviting me to be a part of this series, Catholicity in the Twenty-First Century. Ilia has been both a friend and a mentor since being one of my professors at Washington Theological Union. To be a Christian theologian is to be a part of a tradition that is much larger than oneself. To quote Paul, "I have handed on to you what I myself have been given." In that sense this book is absolutely indebted to another of my professors at Washington Theological Union, Donald Buggert, O.Carm. Our teachers define us by forming our theological worldview and/or by becoming foils over and against whom we form our own theological worldviews. Don Buggert was primarily the former for me, forming and informing my Rahnerian theological worldview. In my teaching, in my thinking, and in my writing, my words are often his words, and I no longer know where his end and mine begin. Mine would not be possible without his. This book would not be possible without what I have learned and absorbed from him, and his words echo throughout this work.

I would also like to thank my mother, Janie Russell, for tirelessly reading through drafts of chapters. She helped me to shape the overall structure of the book as well as improve its accessibility to a general readership. I also have to thank my father, Dan Russell, for his patience while she spent hours reading those drafts.

I would like to thank the community of students and colleagues at the Institute of Pastoral Studies at Loyola University Chicago for their encouragement and support. I would like to thank Mike Leach and the editorial staff at Orbis Books for their work with the manuscript.

Finally, I would like to thank my children DJ and Ella for being my inspiration and for reminding me constantly that love is a miracle that knows no bounds. In and through them I encounter my God, who is the Source of Love revealed in Word and enacted in Spirit, to whom I owe my very breath and heart.

Foreword

Ilia Delio, OSF

The great twentieth-century German theologian Karl Rahner once remarked that Christians are essentially monists. One could dispense with the doctrine of the Trinity as false, he quipped, and the major part of religious literature could well remain virtually unchanged.[1] Not only the literature, we might add, but the daily practice of Christian life would also be unaffected. The Trinity remains an elusive mystery for most Christians.

Rahner's insight lies behind the classic work of Catherine Mowry LaCugna's *God for Us*. Writing her *magnum opus* in the late twentieth century, LaCugna felt that the theological critiques of the twentieth century, including a God who is sexist, patriarchal, apathetic, and ontologically aloof did not do justice to divine revelation in Jesus Christ. Her retrieval of a living Trinity for our age was not simply to enhance the experience of God but, more so, to elucidate the mystery of God's eternal being. For Christian theology a proper response to revelation must be grounded in trinitarian theology, the view that the Trinity, three Persons in one God, runs through all aspects of theology like gold through a mountain range.[2] Hence, in the first line of her introduction she writes: "The doctrine of the Trinity is ultimately a practical doctrine with radical consequences for Christian life."[3] The adjective *practical* seems to have been carefully chosen; the doctrine of the Trinity is not a speculative theological puzzle but shapes the

---

[1] Karl Rahner, *The Trinity* (New York: Herder and Herder, 1970), 11.

[2] Catherine Mowry LaCugna, *God for Us: The Trinity and Christian Life* (New York: HarperCollins, 1991), 3, 6.

[3] LaCugna, *God for Us*, 1.

entirety of Christian life, from prayer and worship to spiritual formation and ethics.

Now, twenty-five years later, Heidi Russell is renewing our understanding of the Trinity not only as the God of Jesus Christ but as ground and goal of the Big Bang cosmos. Whereas LaCugna began with the historical development of the Trinity, Russell begins her discussion with quantum physics, seeking the ground of an intrinsically relational universe. She focuses in a particular way on physicist David Bohm's idea of implicate order, connoting the undivided wholeness of reality. As human beings and societies we seem separate, but in our roots we are part of an indivisible whole and share in the same cosmic process. The whole, according to Bohm, has endless depth and movement, and he comes very close to naming the central whole of the undivided wholeness of nature as God. Russell hones in on this insight from physics and develops her book along the lines of deep relationality: a relational God of undivided wholeness is source and flow of an undivided relational universe—an implicate order of wholeness.

Although physicists have yet to agree on what holds the whole together, Russell looks to the Christian revelation of God as love and explores love as the depth, breadth, length, and width of an expanding universe, the unifying energy that drives everything toward greater unity. Love is personal, relational, self-communicative, self-gifting, unitive, and creative. God *is* love (1 Jn 4:18) and, as Michael Meerson, rector of Christ the Savior Orthodox Church in New York, writes:

> God's ultimate reality cannot be located in substance (what it is in itself) but only in personhood: what God is toward another. God exists as the mystery of persons in communion. God exists hypostatically in freedom and ecstasies. Only in communion can God be what God is, and only in communion can God be at all. . . . Since love produces communion among persons, love causes God to be who God is.[4]

"Love causes God to be who God is"—personal, communal, relational, dynamically pouring out love into created reality as Source, Word, and Spirit of Love. If we consider love as the core energy of

---

[4] Michael Aksionov Meerson, *The Trinity of Love in Modern Russian Theology* (Quincy, IL: Franciscan Press, 1998), 4.

the universe, as Pierre Teilhard de Chardin suggested, then relationship and openness to more being and life are the core constituents of cosmic life. The title Trinity describes the expansive breath of divine love embracing, sustaining, and creatively drawing all life into the fullness of unity in love. In Teilhard's words: "Driven by the forces of love, the fragments of the world [continuously] seek each other so that the world may come to being."[5] For the Triune God is not a symmetrical God, a God of perfect balance and control; rather, the "threeness" of God is the asymmetry of divine love, which is deeply personal, present, and faithful, yet open to creativity and future. The Triune God is not a static noun but an energetic verbing of the universe: Trinity "trinitizes" the universe by drawing what is isolated and separate into greater unity and being. God is the incomprehensible wellspring of love at the heart of an expanding universe. The beauty of the asymmetrical Triune God is that divine mystery eludes the human grasp of knowledge that seeks to control, manipulate, or resist God. God is always the more of anything that exists because the nature of love is to be open to more love and thus to more being and life. Trinity defines the openness of God to newness. The Dominican mystic Meister Eckhart intuited this deep mystery of Trinity when he wrote that God is the newest thing there is, the youngest thing, and when we are united to God, we become new again.

Today, science and technology show that nature is not clearly defined or bounded; nature can be created and extended through the *techne* into new forms and mediums. Artificial intelligence has afforded the exploration of nature's plasticity or inherent ability to be reshaped, revealing that nature is not fixed but is a process constituted by the drive for transcendence. What we thought was fixed and bounded is now seen to be permeable and unbounded. Nature can be reshaped, merged with an artifice or animal and reclaimed along new lines of informational flow and relationality, open to new forms. Cyborgs are hybrid entities that are neither wholly technology nor completely organic. If the symbol of the cyborg defines the fluidity of the human person, then it also defines the person of Jesus Christ, indicating that we do not have a clearly defined, exhaustive concept of humanity, let alone divinity. The Christian God is so contrary to

[5] Pierre Teilhard de Chardin, *The Phenomenon of Man*, trans. Bernard Wall (New York: Harper & Row, 1959), 264.

common sense that it destabilizes reified categories. Deliberately showing up as a hybrid creature (divinity and humanity), Jesus reveals the arbitrariness and constructed nature of what is considered the norm. When the divine Word becomes flesh (incarnation), God transcends the boundaries of separation (between divinity and creation) to become something new. God enters into bounded existence, yet these boundaries are not fixed; nature constantly transcends itself in pursuit of new, more unified life symbolized by the resurrection of Jesus Christ. The life of Jesus reveals the inner depth of nature to be protean, open to God, and thus open to hybridization, to becoming something new. No one person or existent can exhaust the presence of God because God is always the more of anything that exists.

Russell explores and illuminates this deep, dynamic Trinity of love. Using insights from modern science, she indicates that it is time to awaken to the centrality of love, not only in human life, but in this unfolding and expanding universe. The indivisible whole, according to Russell, is the living God, flowing from love into love unto the fullness of love. This newness of divine creating love is what catholicity is about, a consciousness of belonging to the whole, grounded in love, and participating in the emerging unity of the whole by living in love. God, as the power of love within the evolving universe, empowers cosmic life to become more whole and unified in love. Like LaCugna, Russell seeks an authentic understanding of God faithful to divine revelation in Jesus Christ by exploring the newness of divine love in a scientific age and the implications of love for Christian life. To live in *this* God impels us to change how we think and act toward one another and in relation to the earth. For the living Triune God is the heartbeat of the universe, pulsating the universe toward ultimate wholeness; it is the God of Jesus Christ, ever ancient, ever new, the power of the future inviting us to expand our souls into a new world.

Introduction

Many people today have a concept of Trinity that can be caricatured as "two men and a bird." In fact, if you do a Google image search for Trinity, you will discover a multitude of images that do depict two men and a bird. In the twenty-first century a new understanding of Trinity must be found that allows Christians to reconcile their image of God with a contemporary, scientific worldview. Theology needs to move away from concrete images of God in which God is pictured as an old man in the sky. The use of concepts such as being and person in our trinitarian theology have too often led to an understanding of God as *a* being or *a* person, or worse as three beings or three persons. Shifting from language of being and person to a concept of God as Love can help counteract this tendency to make God in our own image.

The primary analogy for God as Trinity offered in this book is Source of Love, Word of Love, and Spirit of Love. God the Father is the Unoriginate Source of Love, simply meaning the ultimate source, the source that has no origin itself because it is the origin of all love that exists. That Source of all love has been revealed in the Word of Love. The world was created in and through that Word of Love, and that Word of Love has been spoken into the world in the person of Jesus of Nazareth. The Source of Love is also continually enacted in the Spirit of Love, which is present in the world and active in the heart of all believers forming the Christian community into the body of Christ. As the body of Christ, this community is then called to be the ongoing presence of God as Love in the world. In other words, when people come into contact with the Christian community, they should experience God as Love in that encounter.

These trinitarian images can be further developed in light of the physicist David Bohm's concept of reality as implicate wholeness, meaning a wholeness that is implied or conveyed in each and every part. For Bohm, the relationship of the whole to the parts, or what he calls subwholes, is not that the whole is simply the collection or sum of all the parts. Rather, the whole creates and organizes the parts in such a way that the order (or design) of the whole is enfolded in each part, or dwells in the core of the very being of each part. The whole then unfolds itself in and through all of the parts, and as each part unfolds its own independent yet interconnected existence, it participates in the unfolding of the whole.

To use Bohm's concept as an analogy for God, God is the whole. That whole creates and organizes the entire universe, including each of us. Created in and through the Word, that whole we call God is enfolded into each of our hearts. As we live out our Christian lives in union with that Spirit, that Spirit unfolds or enacts God as Love in the world through us. Bohm's concept of implicate order gives us an image to help us understand God's active, creative, loving presence in and throughout the cosmos, creating an emerging world that both enfolds the very presence of God and unfolds or reveals that love and wholeness as it emerges. As part of that emerging cosmos, created in the image of God, humankind is called to ever greater catholicity, ever greater wholeness, universality, and love.

In her introduction to *Making All Things New*, Ilia Delio describes catholicity as coming "from a Greek word, *katholikos*, which means 'of the whole' or 'a sense of wholeness.' It is the orientation of all life toward making wholes and thus toward universality or turning together as one."[1] The catholicity of our lives is grounded in the Trinity. In the Trinity we find the wholeness that expresses itself in diversity and the diversity that enfolds wholeness. Catholicity is participation in the work of the Trinity, the work of enfolding and unfolding wholeness and love in creation. Our understanding of Trinity must have an implication for the way we understand the world and justice in the world today. Our focus must shift from a culture of individuality and competition to a vision of an interconnected whole in which the suffering of any part of creation has an effect on the whole, thus changing the way we operate as a human society in our relationships with one another, with the created world, and with our God, who is the source of our love and wholeness.

Wholeness is Love. Each of us is a participation and a reflection of that Love, created in its image and likeness. We come from the

[1] Ilia Delio, *Making All Things New: Catholicity, Cosmology, Consciousness* (Maryknoll, NY: Orbis Books, 2015), xi.

Source of Love formed in the Word of Love by the Spirit of Love. That Love becomes incarnate in Christ, and, by the power of the Holy Spirit, we are united in Love to Christ and given back over to the Source of Love.

This book explores the work of scientists, philosophers, and theologians. The wholeness of physicist David Bohm is the Love of philosopher and theologian Jean-Luc Marion as well as Maximus the Confessor. Jesuit theologian Karl Rahner shows that the Love revealed in the economic Trinity (God for us), seen in the structure of the cosmos itself according to both Bohm and Maximus, is the self-communication of the immanent Trinity (God in Godself). My intention at the outset was to construct this book in a traditional sense, beginning with scripture, moving through the patristics, to then conclude with the contemporary thinkers and scientists. Instead, I have chosen to begin with the work of the physicists David Bohm and Lee Smolin. The physicists articulate the way in which the cosmos itself can be understood as an interconnected whole. That implicate wholeness and inherent relationality of the cosmos gives us an analogy to speak of the God whom we believe created the cosmos. From there I explore what I see as the main paradigm shift from Being to Love grounded in the work of Jean-Luc Marion and how it informs a trinitarian theology of Love as Source, Word, and Spirit. Having set that framework for our discussion, we then go back to the beginning to ground this image of Trinity in the monotheism of scripture and the theological development of the tradition.

Chapter 1 investigates the concept of catholicity as wholeness of love in light of physicist David Bohm's concept of implicate order and physicist Lee Smolin's insight into reality as relationality. These images of wholeness and relationality are foundational for our exploration of Trinity as Source of Love revealed in Word and enacted in Spirit. Bohm's understanding of the wholeness of the implicate order enfolded in every part or subwhole and then unfolded in a unique way according to the context in which it is unfolded will be associated with the way in which the Word or Logos enfolds the wholeness of Love into all of creation. That enfolded wholeness of Love is then unfolded through the action of the Spirit forming us into the body of Christ, the ongoing unfolding of Love in the world. It is precisely in and as the body of Christ that we experience and live our catholicity, our wholeness as love in the world.

Chapter 2 grounds the movement away from the language of Persons in the Trinity to the language of Love as Source, Word, and Spirit in Jean-Luc Marion's analogical shift from Being to Love. Using Marion's work, I suggest a similar shift from Person to Love in understanding the Trinity as a way that will address some contemporary critiques of trinitarian theology. This chapter then develops the analogical description of the Trinity as Source, Word, and Spirit of Love.

Chapter 3 explores the scriptural foundations of our monotheism, beginning with the Hebrew scriptures. It then looks at the ways in which the early Christian writers used the images of the Hebrew scriptures, such as Word, Wisdom, and Power, to articulate their experience of Christ and the Spirit in a way that stayed within the bounds of monotheism rather than developing into tritheism. The chapter also touches on the root meanings of the terms *Father* and *Son* to expand this meaning beyond our concrete image of two human beings.

Chapter 4 plumbs the patristic era of theology for trinitarian images that ground our interpretation of God as Source, Word, and Spirit of Love. In this early era of theology God is understood as the unoriginated source who creates through the Word or Logos and is present in the world through the Spirit. Theologians such as Justin, Tertullian, and Athanasius develop rich analogies to articulate the Trinity. Saint Irenaeus of Lyons describes the Son and the Spirit as the "two hands of God" reaching down into the world and connects the concepts of creation and incarnation. The Cappadocians and Maximus the Confessor introduce the idea of perichoresis as interrelationship connecting creation, deification, and incarnation. All of these theologians offer insight into the analogy of God as the unoriginated Source of Love revealed and expressed in the Word and enacted and unfolded in the Spirit.

Chapter 5 explores the way in which the twentieth-century Jesuit theologian Karl Rahner understands Trinity as revealed in incarnation and grace. This chapter explores the concept of incarnation, meaning God's presence in and through Jesus of Nazareth, literally the enfleshing of God. It also explores the concept of grace as the presence of the Holy Spirit in the heart of every person, pouring out the offer of God's love and presence into each human heart.

Chapter 6 looks more intently at the critiques and claims of the social analogy of the Trinity, focusing on Jürgen Moltmann, Leonardo Boff, and Catherine Mowry LaCugna. In addressing the idea that we can define what it means to be a human person by looking at the Persons of the Trinity, Chapter 6 suggests an alternative turn to the human person of Jesus Christ as the model for human personhood. Likewise, rather than turn to the Trinity as the ideal image of community, we discover what it means to be a community in the Spirit-formed community of the Acts of the Apostles.

Chapter 7 concludes with a discussion of how catholicity as the wholeness of Love addresses the issues of fragmentation in this world. The response of the Triune God to sin is not wrath but love, which is revealed in the crucifixion and resurrection. Hence, how we understand the crucifixion must change to reflect a God of love rather than a God of anger. We look specifically to the ways in which Pope Francis has called us to respond to a world of fragmentation by living out our catholicity in the world, calling us to recognize the wholeness and interconnectedness of all creation.

The Source of All Love

Chapter 1

Enfolded Wholeness—Creation and Trinity

Physicist David Bohm is not a theologian and has no theory of the Trinity. What he does add to our conversation is a theory of wholeness that can be used as a lens for understanding the Trinity and catholicity. Lee Smolin is a physicist who focuses on relationality as being at the core of reality. In both of these scientific theories we find a congruence with a "catholic" worldview that is grounded in the Trinity. In this chapter we first spend some time exploring the scientific theories and then look at the theological implications of these theories. As noted in the Introduction, *catholicity* means "wholeness," and in connection with our analogy of the Trinity as Source, Word, and Spirit of Love, we can further say that catholicity is the wholeness of love. For those of us who are believers in the Triune God of Love, it is no surprise that the natural created world might reflect the wholeness and relationality of the God who is wholeness and relationality.

David Bohm's Vision of Wholeness and Implicate Order

David Bohm's understanding of reality, in which wholeness is at the core of our experience, can be used to reimagine the Trinity as enfolded and unfolding in all of creation. Bohm notes that we have an intuitive understanding of reality as wholeness. He ponders:

> Even as a child I was fascinated by the puzzle, indeed the mystery, of what is the nature of movement. Whenever one *thinks* of anything, it seems to be apprehended either as static,

> or as a series of static images. Yet, in the actual experience of movement, one *senses* an unbroken, undivided process of flow, to which the series of static images in thought is related as a series of "still" photographs might be related to the actuality of a speeding car.[1]

When we analyze an event, we tend to break experiences into pieces, but when we live, we live as if reality is an unbroken whole.

Despite our almost automatic assumption of wholeness, Bohm points out that we live lives of fragmentation. From a theological perspective this fragmentation can obscure the wholeness at the core of creation and can be seen as humanity's original sin. Reflecting on the "general problem of fragmentation of human consciousness," Bohm suggests that

> the widespread and pervasive distinctions between people (race, nation, family, profession, etc., etc.), which are now preventing mankind from working together for the common good, and indeed, even for survival, have one of the key factors of their origin in a kind of thought that treats things as inherently divided, disconnected, and "broken up" into yet smaller constituent parts. Each part is considered to be essentially independent and self-existent.[2]

Bohm explains that what is a useful way of *thinking* about things, that is, breaking things up into smaller parts, has been mistaken with actuality or reality.

In other words, what has been a useful tool is now an obstacle to our understanding the undivided wholeness of reality. Our US culture is at a point where fragmentation and division have gridlocked our political system and created division among neighbors, friends, and families. We focus on what divides us rather than seeing our neighbor as part of our own wholeness. An electronic age in which people can anonymously write scathing comments, hurling insults at one another from behind the safety of their computer screens, has ripped open the wounds of racism, classism, and sexism in our culture. Bohm

---

[1] David Bohm, *Wholeness and the Implicate Order* (London: Routledge, 2002), x.

[2] Ibid., xii.

notes that both the English words *health* and *holy* stem from the word *whole,* so that searching for wholeness amid the fragmentation we have imposed on reality is part of the human quest for meaning.[3] Only when we prioritize our catholicity, our wholeness in love, will we be able to move beyond the gridlock of fragmentation as a people, a society, and a church.

Wholeness in the Realm of Science

Two realms of science suggest an underlying wholeness to reality, relativity and quantum theory. Both relativity and quantum theory have had to acknowledge that the world is not simply made up of smaller and smaller building blocks that fit together to make the larger whole. From quantum mechanics we learn that reality unites observer and observed. From relativity we learn that "one has to view the world in terms of universal flux of events and processes."[4] One of the great challenges of science today is to integrate these two theories of relativity and quantum mechanics. Bohm explains this quandary of trying to reconcile the two: "relativity theory requires continuity, strict causality (or determinism) and locality. On the other hand, quantum theory requires noncontinuity, noncausality and nonlocality. So the basic concepts of relativity and quantum theory directly contradict each other."[5] Bohm suggests that in order to reconcile the two theories, one must begin with what they have in common, which is undivided wholeness.[6]

In quantum mechanics Bohm has differed from the usual Copenhagen interpretation, which suggests that particle wave complementarity means that the state of a subatomic "particle" (which is to say, whether it is behaving as a particle or a wave) is dependent on the observer, or perhaps more accurately, the device used to measure the particle. Put more simply, if your experiment asks "wave" questions, you get "wave" responses. If your experiment asks "particle" questions, you get "particle" responses. Subatomic particles display properties of both particles and waves depending on the experiment.

---

[3] Ibid., 3–4.
[4] Ibid., 12.
[5] Ibid., 223.
[6] Ibid.

Another way of stating this point is that you cannot know both the position and the momentum of a particle simultaneously. The double-slit experiment with electrons demonstrated this point, as does the famous thought experiment of Schrödinger's Cat. Particles (or the cat) exist in states of superposition, meaning that until the measurement takes place, they can be or are in any and all of the possible positions. The Copenhagen interpretation uses probability in its equations, so that the electron could be anywhere, but it is more probable that it will be in some places than in others, and the extreme possibilities cancel one another out. Nonetheless, any of the states of the electron are possible, even if not very probable.[7] Timothy Murphy explains:

> In the Copenhagen interpretation of quantum physics, buttressed by Heisenberg's own indeterminacy principle, the statistical structure of the equations makes it meaningless to ask what happens to a particle or field between observations; therefore it is meaningless to claim that the particle or field exists when it is not being observed. All that *is*, all that has meaning, is the mathematical expression of probabilities.[8]

The Copenhagen interpretation is not concerned with the philosophy of quantum physics or the questions about what is happening to the particle or where it is when it is not being observed. The concern is utility. The mathematical equations need to work and be able to be used for practical purposes. The theory has been immensely successful in that regard. Theorists using this interpretation generally do not concern themselves with how or why it works. They simply use the theory for practical applications.

---

[7] For a much more detailed account of these theories of quantum mechanics see Heidi Russell, *Quantum Shift: Theological and Pastoral Implications of Contemporary Developments in Science* (Collegeville, MN: Liturgical Press, 2015); Heidi Russell, "Quantum Anthropology: Reimaging the Human Person as Body/Spirit," *Theological Studies* 74, no. 4 (December 2013): 934–59.

[8] Timothy S. Murphy, "Quantum Ontology: A Virtual Mechanics of Becoming," in *Deleuze and Guattari: New Mappings in Politics, Philosophy, and Culture,* ed. Eleanor Kaufman and Kevin Jon Heller (Minneapolis: University of Minnesota Press, 1998), 212.

Not all theorists are content with this state of unknowing, however. Ted Peters summarizes Bohm's issue with this interpretation:

> The problem is that at present there is no consistent notion at all of what the reality might be that underlies the universal constitution and structure of matter. Quantum physicists tend to avoid the issue by concentrating on mathematical equations that permit us to predict and control the behavior of large statistical aggregates of particles, while adopting an attitude that any overall view of the nature of reality is of little or no importance.[9]

Murphy goes on to explain:

> A number of contemporary physicists, including Roger Penrose, J. S. Bell, and David Bohm, have attempted to formulate a consistent and useful method of treating quantum mechanical events as actual occurrences rather than as probabilities that fulfill formal equations (and nothing else); chief among these was the late David Bohm, who made a concerted effort to formulate not only a new method of treating quantum equations but also a realist ontological framework into which to contextualize the mathematics.[10]

Bohm, among others, does want to concern us with a comprehensive view of reality. He asks the burning questions of what is really happening and where is the electron when it is not being observed or measured. Our inquiring minds want to know, and given our own experience of reality, there is the sense that when the electron is not being observed, it must be somewhere, not everywhere or nowhere.

As an alternative to the Copenhagen interpretation, David Bohm's hidden variable interpretation postulates an unknown field or potential called the quantum potential, which is undetectable or hidden due to the way in which we do our experiments.[11] In this theory the electrons

---

[9] Ted Peters, "David Bohm, Postmodernism, and the Divine," *Zygon* 20, no. 2 (1985): 197.

[10] Murphy, "Quantum Ontology," 213.

[11] Robert John Russell, "The Physics of David Bohm and Its Relevance to Philosophy and Theology," *Zygon* 20, no. 2 (1985): 138.

do have precisely determined trajectories guided by this quantum field or potential that is as of yet undetectable. To summarize the difference between the two interpretations of quantum mechanics in another way, David Albert explains the Copenhagen interpretation:

> First, pure chance governs the innermost workings of nature. Second, although material objects always occupy space, situations exist in which they occupy no particular region of space. Third and perhaps most surprising, the fundamental laws that govern the behaviors of "ordinary" physical objects somehow fail to apply to objects that happen to be functioning as "measuring instruments" or "observers."[12]

Albert then goes on to explain that in David Bohm's theory "chance plays no role at all, and every material object invariably does occupy some particular region of space. Moreover, this theory takes the form of a single set of basic physical laws that apply in exactly the same way to every physical object that exists."[13] On this third point the Copenhagen interpretation would say that anything smaller than a Planck measurement acts according to quantum laws whereas anything larger acts according to Newton's laws. For Bohm, the quantum laws can be explained according to Newton's laws, if one postulates the existence of these hidden variables, the wave function as a field and quantum potential.

There are many different schools of interpretation about the meaning of the results of these experiments. The Copenhagen interpretation and the hidden variables theory are just two of them. The Copenhagen interpretation is the most commonly accepted theory among physicists today. The hidden variables theory is perhaps the least accepted. Field and string theories are two additional ways of interpreting the data from these experiments. Theologians must be a little cautious in utilizing these theories that are less popular in the scientific world, lest we seem out of touch with contemporary theories, but at the same time, the fact that a theory does not currently enjoy wide acceptance does not rule it out as a possibility, as

---

[12] David Z. Albert, "Bohm's Alternative to Quantum Mechanics," *Scientific American*, no. 270 (May 1994): 58.

[13] Ibid.

the history (not to mention the multiple theories) of quantum physics clearly demonstrates!

David Bohm's implicate order is not a concept that is generally accepted by most physicists who either still operate out of the Copenhagen interpretation or see explanations such as the many worlds theory as being more attractive than hidden variables. While Bohm worked out mathematical equations for the concept of the advanced and retarded waves within his theory, there is no scientific proof or possible way to test for the existence of the hidden variables or what Bohm calls super quantum potential. However, were Bohm living today, he would most likely point out that there is currently no proof or possible way to test for the existence of strings in string theory either, and yet many scientists today are focusing their efforts and theories in that direction.

In other words, at issue is the fact that there are multiple ways of interpreting this data and devising mathematical formulas to explain the data, but right now it is impossible to prove any of the theories; some (primarily the Copenhagen school) would maintain that it is not that we do not yet have the capability of proving or disproving these theories, but that what we are discussing is inherently impossible to prove or disprove.

David Bohm's Interpretation of the Double Slit Experiment

As David Bohm summarizes the problem of the double slit experiment, "a detector will detect an electron in some small region of space, while the extended spherical wave gives only the probability that it will be found in any such region."[14] In other words, when one observes or measures the location of the particle, it behaves as one expects a particle to behave and is found in a specific place. When one is not observing or measuring the particle directly, it behaves like a wave, creating an interference pattern on the detection screen.

David Bohm's concept of implicate order speculates that there is a second wave, an ingoing wave corresponding to the outgoing wave that has what he names quantum potential, and that this wave is an

[14] David Bohm, "Hidden Variables and the Implicate Order," *Zygon* 20, no. 2 (1985): 113.

independent actuality that has an impact on the so-called particle. The incoming wave reflects the whole environment and the effect of the whole on the part. Bohm has developed mathematical equations that show this to be a possibility, though one that has not and perhaps cannot be proven or disproven through physical experiments. In Bohm's interpretation of quantum mechanics, the wave function is not just a wave of probability, as the Copenhagen interpretation suggests, but represents "an objectively real field and not just a mathematical symbol."[15] This field "is actually in a state of very rapid and random chaotic fluctuation" so that its values "are a kind of average over a characteristic interval of time."[16] This wave/field is sometimes called a pilot wave, because it "pilots" or directs the movement of the particle.

We have no way at present to observe directly Bohm's hypothetical wave field or quantum potential, so his theory is referred to as a hidden variables theory. The wave field and the quantum potential are variables that are at present hidden or unobservable but may be detectable one day in the future as we develop new devices of measurement. Bohm compares the theory to that of Brownian motion, by which atoms were first detected before we had equipment capable of directly observing them.[17] In more technical terms, he explains:

> The intensity of this wave is proportional to the probability that a particle actually is in the corresponding region of space (and is not merely the probability of our observing the phenomena involved in finding a particle there). So the wave function had a double interpretation—first, as a function from which the quantum potential could be derived, and second, as a function from which probabilities could be derived.
>
> From these assumptions, one was able to show that all the usual results of the quantum theory could be obtained on the basis of a model incorporating the independent actuality of all its basic elements (field and particle), as well as an in-principle complete causal determination of the behavior of these elements in terms of all the relevant equations (at least

---

[15] Bohm, *Wholeness and the Implicate Order*, 98.

[16] Ibid.

[17] Ibid., 98–99.

> in a one-particle system, which is as far as [Bohm] had gotten at the time).[18]

Put more simply, John Horgan explains:

> In Bohm's view, a quantum entity such as an electron does in fact exist in a particular place at a particular time, but its behavior is governed by an unusual field, or pilot wave, whose properties are defined by the Schrodinger wave function. The hypothesis does allow one quantum quirk, nonlocality, but it eliminates another, the indefiniteness of position of a particle. Its predictions are identical to those of standard quantum mechanics.[19]

This incoming or advanced wave (a wave going in towards and converging upon the electron instead of flowing out from the electron) with its quantum potential is not separate from the outgoing or retarded wave but rather intimately interconnected with it. Bohm's thinking about the incoming wave with its quantum potential that was able to communicate to the electron information about the whole of reality led to Bohm's later theories about wholeness as the implicate order of reality itself.

---

[18] Bohm, "Hidden Variables and the Implicate Order," 114. It is worth noting at this point that Louis de Broglie had come up with a similar interpretation of the double slit experiment. Neither man's theory has been disproven; both provide the same experimental results as the standard interpretation; and yet they are not generally utilized in mainstream physics. Bohm suggests: "If de Broglie's ideas had won the day at the Solvay Congress of 1927, they might have become the accepted interpretation. Then if someone had come along to propose the current interpretation, one could equally well have said that, since, after all, it gave no new experimental results, there would be no point in considering it seriously. In other words, I felt that the adoption of the current interpretation was a somewhat fortuitous affair, since it was affected not only by the outcome of the Solvay Conference, but also by the generally positivist empiricist attitude that pervaded physics at the time. This attitude is in many ways even stronger today and shows up in the fact that a model that gives insight without an 'empirical pay-off cannot be taken seriously'" (116). See also Albert, "Bohm's Alternative to Quantum Mechanics," 58–67; John Horgan, "Quantum Philosophy," *Scientific American* 267 (1992): 94–104.

[19] Horgan, "Quantum Philosophy," 104.

A Changing Worldview

Our very ways of thinking, of ordering our perception of the world around us, influence the way in which we think about or understand God. David Bohm explores how the ways in which we order the world around us influence physics and our perception of reality. Bohm describes the history of how we have ordered our understanding of the universe beginning with the ancient Greeks who saw the universe as a living organism organized in a pattern of epicycles or circles within circles.[20] Bohm notes that rather than change one's sense of order to account for new observations, the old system is continuously "adjusted" to make the new observations fit the prevailing order until eventually a paradigm shift occurs to an entirely new way of thinking about order.[21] With Copernicus, Galileo, Kepler, and Newton, such a shift happens in which the earth is understood to revolve around the sun instead of vice versa, and the universe is imaged as a machine rather than an organism in which the parts are understood to be separate, but working together.[22] Ted Peters nicely summarizes the Newtonian worldview that was overturned by relativity and quantum mechanics:

> The world view which constitutes the framework of Newtonian physics is based upon the three dimensional space of Euclidean geometry and the notion of the mathematically calculable and constantly reliable flow of time from past to future. In this receptacle of absolute space and time there moves material elements or particles, the small, solid, and ultimately indestructible objects out of which all matter is made. These material atomic units can be located in space and time. Their velocity and size can be measured. They are basically passive, their relationships to one another being determined by external forces of nature such as gravity. These forces or laws of motion presume a closed causal nexus or mechanistic structure. Any definite cause gives rise to a definite effect, and the future of any part of the world system could be, in principle, predicted with certainty should one know the details of the causes. This leads to the image of the world as a machine, to an implicit and rigorous mechanical determinism.[23]

---

[20] Bohm, *Wholeness and the Implicate Order*, 142–43.

[21] Ibid., 143.

[22] Ibid., 144.

[23] Peters, "David Bohm, Postmodernism, and the Divine," 195.

In other words, in the Newtonian system we were able to understand reality by breaking it up into its constituent parts. Everything existed in a specific place and time, and we could observe interactions between the parts in the process of cause and effect. When I push the ball, it rolls. This new schema was further ordered by Cartesian coordinates, achieved by using a grid "constituted of three perpendicular sets of uniformly spaced lines."[24] In the Newtonian system it was commonly believed that we would be able to predict everything, if we only had all of the data to enter into the equations.

With the advent of Einstein's theory of relativity, with the insight that the speed of light is constant, this stable grid was suddenly understood to warp and weave, and therefore time and space must adjust to maintain that constant (the faster you move through space, the slower you move through time and vice versa).[25] Furthermore, this fabric of space and time was affected by gravity, so that space itself was understood to be warped by the mass of objects like planets. Spacetime was suddenly understood as a whole in which one part is affected by another. Along with this new conception of reality, Einstein introduced field theory, in which the particle is understood as an intense pulse within the field as opposed to an individual object.[26] Bohm concludes:

> So, in terms of this notion, the idea of a separately and independently existent particle is seen to be, at best, an abstraction furnishing a valid approximation only in a certain limited domain. Ultimately, the entire universe (with all its particles, including those constituting human beings, their laboratories, observing instruments, etc.) has to be understood as a single undivided

[24] Bohm, *Wholeness and the Implicate Order*, 144.

[25] Think of the fact that even when you are sitting still (which, mind you, you are never actually doing, because the earth is moving), you are still moving through time. Our variances in speed are not great enough to affect our movement through time. Only if we were able to achieve speeds close to the speed of light would we notice a difference between how a person traveling at the speed of light experiences time compared to how one remaining on earth experiences time. Note that for the person traveling near the speed of light, there would be no noticeable change in time. The difference can only be experienced in comparison to another person not traveling near the speed of light.

[26] Bohm, *Wholeness and the Implicate Order,* 220.

> whole, in which analysis into separately and independently existent parts has no fundamental status.[27]

In the new worldview, there is no longer any such thing as a separate, disconnected individual. All that exists is relationship and wholeness. The cosmos is catholicity.

David Bohm's Implicate Order

In taking wholeness as primary and actual from the discoveries of relativity and quantum mechanics, David Bohm articulates what he calls implicate or implicit order, in which the order of the whole is enfolded into each part, or what Bohm prefers to call subwhole. He suggests that in reality there is both an implicate order and an explicate order. We see and experience the explicate order in our everyday lives. The implicate order, however, is both hidden and yet more primary than the explicate order. We don't "see" the implicate order, and yet it is at the core of reality and unfolded in the explicate order of our everyday experience. Thus, for Bohm, the implicate order, which is the hidden order of the whole, is fundamental. The explicate order, that which we see and experience, "is only a particularly distinguished case of the implicate order."[28] The implicate order is enfolded into each subwhole. Bohm uses the image of poking a hole through a piece of paper that has been folded many times. Imagine making paper snowflakes as a child. When the paper is unfolded, a complex pattern appears. The complex pattern is unfolded into the explicate order from the implicate order by which it was created.[29] In a similar way Bohm suggests that the hidden implicate order is enfolded into each part of the explicate order that we see. Each subwhole exists within the

---

[27] Ibid., 221. While field theory has changed the way in which we understand particle physics, Bohm also points out that Einstein was not able to solve ultimately the problems of physics with this theory (160–61; 221). Furthermore, even field theory still operates by a mechanistic understanding of the universe as the fields themselves are understood to be separate entities that only affect each other through external or local causal relationships (221).

[28] Bohm, "Hidden Variables and the Implicate Order," 118.

[29] David Bohm, "Fragmentation and Wholeness in Religion and in Science," *Zygon* 20, no. 2 (1985): 129.

whole, and the whole exists in each subwhole. The enfolded implicate order that is in each subwhole is then unfolded into our everyday reality in the same way that the pattern of the snowflake appears when we unfold our piece of paper.

Bohm's favorite analogy for explaining enfolded wholeness is a hologram. A regular lens or photograph creates a point-by-point correspondence between the object and the two-dimensional image of the object that is created. A hologram, however, creates a three-dimensional image by having each point of the image contain the whole of the image. Bohm explains: "The form and structure of the entire object may be said to be *enfolded* within each region of the photographic record. When one shines light on any region, this form and structure are then *unfolded* to give a recognizable image of the whole object once again."[30] Bohm suggests, "The word 'implicit' is based on the verb 'to implicate'. This means 'to fold inward' (as multiplication means 'folding many times'). So we may be led to explore the notion that in some sense each region [of space and time] contains a total structure 'enfolded' within it."[31] Bohm explains using the example of a television signal, in which "the visual image is translated into a time order, which is 'carried' by the radio wave. . . . Thus, the radio wave carries the visual image in an implicate order. The function of the receiver is then to *explicate* this order, i.e., to 'unfold' it in the form of a new visual image."[32] Note that in both of these examples an external element, the light for the hologram and the receiver for the radio wave, catalyzes the unfolding of the enfolded whole.

In addition to the example of the hologram as a way of explaining the relationship between implicate and explicate order, Bohm uses the image of a seed, which contains the whole of the plant, which in turn contains more seeds and is part of a larger system called a forest.[33] The forest is enfolded in the seed, and yet that seed is unique within the forest. This image demonstrates analogously the way in which the enfolded whole makes one part of a larger interconnected

---

[30] Bohm, *Wholeness and the Implicate Order*, 225.

[31] Ibid., 188.

[32] Ibid.

[33] David Bohm, "The Implicate Order: A New Approach to the Nature of Reality," in *Beyond Mechanism: The Universe in Recent Physics and Catholic Thought*, ed. Davie Schindler (Lanham, MD: University Press of America, 1986), 27–28.

system while also enabling one to have a relatively unique and autonomous existence.

Another image Bohm uses to explain the concept of wholeness and implicate order is water and the way in which it moves and flows. He uses the image of a stream or river, where one can see on the surface of the water the pattern of vortices. The vortices may develop a quite stable pattern of existence, but they are always part of the greater whole and interconnected with the entirety of the stream, affected by all of the other movements and patterns within it. He explains:

> One may here use the image of a set of vortices on a fluid, such as water. Each vortex is a pattern of movement—one that is stable and recurrent, but nonetheless, just a form in the movement of the fluid as a whole. Such a form may be abstracted in the mind as if it were a separately existent vortex, but actually it has no such separate existence. The movement patterns of two or more vortices merge and fuse, with no sharp breaks between them. This gives some notion of how the so-called elementary particles are to be regarded as abstract patterns of movement in a field, covering the entire universe. Since this suggests that the whole is a primary notion, while the parts are abstractions from the whole, the traditional mechanistic notion of the constitution of the world out of separately existent parts is turned upside down.[34]

Because the pattern is stable and weakens with distance from the center, it can be viewed as a relatively independent entity, but in fact it is connected to the whole, a point that is illustrated when it is brought into proximity with a second vortex.[35] When the two are far apart, they interact weakly, but when brought together, they affect one another strongly and will eventually merge.[36] Bohm suggests that particles are like vortices in a field of unbroken wholeness. Bohm takes the idea of the flowing movement of an unbroken field and combines it with the nonlocal nature of quantum connection. He explains:

---

[34] Bohm, "Fragmentation and Wholeness in Religion and in Science," 128.

[35] Bohm, "The Implicate Order," 17.

[36] Ibid.

> This means that all parts of the universe are connected by indivisible links, so that there is no way ultimately to divide the world into independently existent parts (in principle, this extends even to the observer and what is observed). Moreover, the fundamental nature of each part (wave or particle) depends inextricably on this web of indivisible quantum links that are its context. And finally, since indivisible interconnection may extend even to distant regions of space, it follows that the very nature of each part may depend significantly on what is happening in places that are quite far from it.[37]

Reality is interconnectedness and relationship. Bohm suggests that

> all matter can be seen to describe just such a movement as has been explained above, in which there is continued enfoldment of the whole into each region, along with unfoldment of each region into the whole. Although this may take many particular forms, some of which are now known, and others of which are not, such movement is as we have seen universal.[38]

Bohm concludes:

> The proposal is then that the holomovement is the basic reality, and that all entities, objects, forms, etc., as ordinarily seen are relatively stable, independent and autonomous features of the holomovement (as the vortex is such a feature of the flowing movement of a liquid). The basic order of this movement is therefore enfoldment and unfoldment. So we are looking at the universe in terms of a new order, which we shall call the *enfolded order* or the *implicate order*.[39]

---

[37] Ibid., 20. Bohm makes the distinction between determinism and mechanism. The Copenhagen interpretation has said that quantum mechanics is both nonlocal (not mechanistic) and indeterminate (only probabilities can be determined). Bohm agrees (against Einstein and relativity) that it is nonlocal but differs from the Copenhagen interpretation in suggesting it is deterministic (ibid., 21).

[38] Ibid., 25.

[39] Ibid., 25–26.

Bohm calls "the totality of movement of enfoldment and unfoldment" *holomovement* (as in the quotation above) and summarizes:

> Our basic proposal was then that *what is* is the holomovement, and that everything is to be explained in terms of forms derived from this holomovement. Though the full set of laws governing its totality is unknown (and, indeed, probably unknowable) nevertheless these laws are assumed to be such that from them may be abstracted relatively autonomous or independent sub-totalities of movement (e.g., fields, particles, etc.) having a certain recurrence and stability of their basic patterns of order and measure. Such sub-totalities may then be investigated, each in its own right, without our having first to know the full laws of the holomovement.[40]

He notes that in a mechanistic view, the elements, such as the particles and fields, are primary, the enfoldment and unfoldment are secondary, whereas in his view "the movement of enfolding and unfolding is ultimately the primary reality, and that the objects, entities, forms, etc., which appear in this movement are secondary."[41] The implicate order is the whole of the universe actively folded into each part, and that enfoldment is different in each part and is central to determining what each part *is*.[42]

The Enfolded and Unfolding Source of All Love—The Implicate Order of the Source of Love

How is this theory at all relevant to our understanding of the Trinity and catholicity? Analogously, we can image the Source of Love as the implicate order of wholeness with the Logos as the enfolded holomovement and the Spirit as the unfolding of the holomovement. The Triune God of Love enfolded into our very being is at the core of who we are as persons. The explicate order is the mechanistic or external relationships among the parts (or subwholes). These external

---

[40] Bohm, *Wholeness and the Implicate Order*, 226.

[41] Bohm, "The Implicate Order," 25.

[42] Ibid., 26.

relationships are real, but secondary, "that is to say, the order of the world as a structure of things that are basically external to each other comes out as a secondary order through the activity of unfoldment which emerges from a deeper and more inward implicate order."[43] We experience our connectedness to one another in a mechanistic and external way, which is also to say in a local way. We as individuals relate to and interact with other individuals with whom we come into contact. Following Bohm, we could suggest analogously that through the Spirit indwelling within us (at least as offer, as discussed in Chapter 5), the Triune God at the core of our being connects us to every person who exists, has existed, and will ever exist. Furthermore, it connects us to all creation and most fundamentally to God in Godself. This interconnection is primary, even though it is not necessarily explicit or conscious. The connection is nonlocal, but it undergirds and enables all of our external and explicit relationships.

Bohm describes his approach to wholeness:

> It means, firstly, that we understand this totality as an unbroken and seamless whole, in which each relatively independent and autonomous entity, object, form, etc., merges along with the others, in a background of ultimately immeasureable extension and depth of inwardness. And secondly, it means that insofar as the wholeness is comprehended with the aid of the notion of the implicate order, the ultimate internality of relationship has necessarily to be taken as basic.[44]

In other words, we are grounded in what is whole and immeasurable, and our interrelatedness is what is most basic to our existence. We are grounded in infinity, and that infinity unites us to all of the rest of creation. Bohm argues:

> All that is manifest in the world is to be considered as unfolding from a deeper, more subtle nonmanifest order. In this process, each part of the universe enfolds the whole and therefore it enfolds all the other parts. This enfoldment is active, and not merely passive. That is to say, the movement,

---

[43] Ibid.

[44] Ibid., 33.

> activity, and internal nature of each part is an expression of the whole. The whole thus creates, sustains, and determines its parts (which should perhaps rather be called subwholes). In this way, mechanism is basically denied. But the unfoldment is such that in large areas of experience, the parts behave with relative independence and autonomy. Hence, the world has a mechanical aspect or side. But this is not actually an independent basis. Rather, it arises in unfoldment from an undivided whole.[45]

What is most internal to us and most basic about us is relationship. Relationship to the whole is what we are calling God, and it encompasses our relationship to one another. Catholicity describes the way our individual wholeness depends on our consciousness of our interconnectedness. As Ilia Delio points out, "Catholicity requires an integrated consciousness of the whole, a deep relationality, as well as a deepening of inner and outer wholeness. It calls us to recognize that connectedness is a basic reality of our existence. We are wholes within wholes. All we do affects all the other wholes of which we are a part and all the other parts that make us whole."[46] Increasing our consciousness of our catholicity thus allows us to overcome the illusion of separateness that leads to fragmentation and division.

In Bohm's theory the autonomy and independence of the parts results from their dependence on and relationship to the whole. In this model, the whole has "an independent and prior significance, such that, indeed, the whole may be said to organize the parts."[47] At the same time, this whole creates and organizes subwholes that are able to act as independent elements, but able to do so because they have been created, organized, and empowered by the whole.[48] To mirror an axiom of the theologian Karl Rahner, the autonomy of the subwhole exists in a relationship of direct proportion to the dependence of the subwhole on the whole. Bohm explains:

> Within the holomovement, as we have seen, each part emerges as relatively independent, autonomous, and stable, and it does

---

[45] Bohm, "Fragmentation and Wholeness in Religion and in Science," 129–30.

[46] Ilia Delio, *Making All Things New: Catholicity, Cosmology, Consciousness* (Maryknoll, NY: Orbis Books, 2015), 199.

[47] Bohm, "Hidden Variables and the Implicate Order," 115.

[48] Ibid., 116.

> so by virtue of the particular way in which it *actively* enfolds the whole (and therefore all the other parts). Its fundamental qualities and activities, internal and external, which are essential to what it *is*, are thus understood as determined basically in such internal relationship, rather than in isolation and external interaction. This means, of course, that all parts are internally related, through such relationship with the whole.[49]

In Bohm's words, who we are and our autonomy flow out of our internal relatedness to the whole, and as Bohm explains, for each of us to have the whole enfolded within means that we also have all of the other parts enfolded within. As Bohm says, the parts are related *internally*, which is to say, nonlocally, so our relationships to all others and to creation itself are nonlocal relationships inherent to the enfolded nature of the whole within us. Bohm suggests that "this enfoldment is *active*, in the sense that it enters in a fundamental way into the activities that are essential to what a human being *is*. Each human being is thus internally related to the totality including nature, and the whole of mankind. He is also therefore internally related to other human beings."[50]

While Bohm is not identifying the whole with God, and in fact takes pains to deny such an identification,[51] in our theological

[49] Bohm, "The Implicate Order," 13–37, 33–34.

[50] Ibid., 34.

[51] When using Bohm's ideas to talk about the Trinity, we are using these concepts analogously, not literally. Bohm himself asserts: "The holomovement is not to be considered as divine. Rather, as with all scientific theories, I regard it as inherently incomplete and contingent on that which goes beyond it. If this 'beyond' is carried to an ultimate transcendent, then the main point about the implicate order will be that it provides a much more natural account of how the transcendent is able to act creatively within matter than does a mechanistic approach (i.e., by proceeding from ever more subtle levels of enfoldment outward toward the explicate order)." David Bohm, "Response to Conference Papers on 'David Bohm's Implicate Order, Physics, Philosophy, and Theology,'" *Zygon* 20, no. 2 (1985): 220. While Bohm acknowledges "there is at least an analogy between how the super-implicate order organizes and even forms and creates the first implicate order and the way in which God is regarded as creating the universe (at least as this is put in many religions)," he "would prefer to regard this as no more than an analogy or a metaphor, that may be useful for giving insight, but that should not be taken too literally." Bohm, "Hidden Variables and the Implicate Order," 123.

analogy, the Triune God of Love is the whole that organizes the parts or subwholes. Our wholeness is grounded in the wholeness of God as Love. Similar to Karl Rahner's understanding of human freedom and autonomy existing in direct proportion to dependence on God, a concept to which we will return in Chapter 5, Bohm's subwholes enjoy an independence that exists in direct correlation to their being an interconnected part of the larger whole.

Bohm goes on to explain that while each subwhole, or what he also calls form, is enfolded in the whole and the whole is enfolded in each subwhole, the relationship is one of asymmetry. He elaborates:

> The form [subwhole] enfolds the whole in only a limited and not completely defined way. The way in which the extended form enfolds the whole is however not merely superficial or of secondary significance, but rather it is essential to what that form is and to how it acts, moves, and behaves quite generally. So the whole is, in a deep sense, internally related to the parts. And since the whole unfolds all the parts, these latter are also internally related, though in a weaker way than they are related to the whole.[52]

Analogically, the Source of Love is enfolded into our hearts because we have been created in and through the self-expression of that Love that we call the Word or Logos. That Love is then enacted in the world through the Spirit, who has been poured into our hearts and unfolds that Love in the world in and through us as the body of Christ. The manner in which the Spirit dwells in each of us and unfolds God as Love in and through us is obviously limited and not in a completely defined way, and yet that indwelling is at the core of who we are as persons and how we act, move, and behave quite generally. In other words, while the wholeness of God as Love dwells within us through the Spirit we have been given, we are still limited and finite beings, and that unfolding of Love in and through us is likewise limited. Furthermore, through the enfolded Logos and unfolding Spirit we are not only united to the Source of Love, we are united to one another. We unfold that Love in and through our interconnectedness. Our catholicity or wholeness in love depends on our being community.

[52] Ibid., 118.

Kevin Sharpe suggests that nonlocality is a way to speak about the connectedness that flows from the divine, noting that "everything instantaneously connects with everything else in ways that defy normal explanations. Nonlocality feels like the all-embracing being of God who is omniscient and omnipotent, not restricted by space and time."[53]

Jesuit theologian John Haughey poetically asks: "What Does the Trinity Do When It Is Off Work? It ones—a verb / (don't start partitioning this into participles/or twisting it into tenses) / Their one-ing began with Three from the beginning / and never stops being thus."[54] In Bohm's terms, one could say that the Trinity "wholes." Using Bohm's implicate order to describe the Father as Source of All Love, one can image this Source as

> unbroken wholeness in flowing movement, for in the implicate order the totality of existence is enfolded within each region of space (and time). So, whatever part, element, or aspect we may abstract in thought, this still enfolds the whole and is therefore intrinsically related to the totality from which it has

[53] Kevin J. Sharpe, "Holomovement Metaphysics and Theology," *Zygon* 28, no. 1 (1993): 54. Sharpe suggests two ways in which "theology could use the holomovement idea as a model for God. . . . The weaker is to make the relation between God and the world like that between the holomovement and the arena of human experience. The God-world relation is like the implicate-order-explicate-order relation. While many purposes only need this, others require something stronger; namely, that God is like the holomovement. Exploring the theology of the holomovement God often requires the latter. Second, God contains the world as the implicate contains the explicate. The explicate comes from the implicate and folds back into it; the explicate is a particular part or restriction of the implicate. Further, as the explicate folds back into the implicate, what happens in the explicate order affects the implicate. Thus, the world and human beings can affect God" (55). Sharpe also suggests that there is a correlation both with God as creating ex nihilo (out of nothing) in that the explicate order emerges from the implicate, and God as creating continua or sustaining creation in the continuous unfolding of the implicate order that occurs within the explicate order (55). He notes that we are co-creators in this process as we contribute to the unfolding of the implicate order in the explicate order (55–56).

[54] John Haughey, *A Biography of the Spirit: There Lies the Dearest Freshness Deep Down Things* (Maryknoll, NY: Orbis Books, 2015), entry for Oct. 30.

> been abstracted. Thus, wholeness permeates all that is being discussed, from the very outset.[55]

So the Source of Love is that which is enfolded into all that exists. God as Love grounds and permeates all of creation.

The Son/Word is then the enfolding or ingoing wave, the agent of creation who enfolds the pattern of the Trinity into all that exists. When Bohm applies the concept of implicate order to human consciousness, he suggests:

> Conscious content of thoughts emerges from a greater whole of which we are not fully conscious. And within this whole, there is the further faculty of reason, which determines the subwholes in thoughts, orders, arranges, connects, and organizes them, and in extreme cases, involves the creative perception of new thoughts. Could we not say that this is, in certain ways, like a super-implicate order?[56]

Lee Nichols explains: "This super-implicate order infuses the implicate order of space with active information, which generates various levels of organization, structure, and meaning."[57] As will be seen in Chapter 4 on the patristics, theology has a long tradition of correlating our own ability to reason and order with creation in the Logos, understood as the reason or mind of God and the principle of order in the cosmos. Here again we see an analogous role of the Logos as the agent of creation who orders, arranges, connects, and organizes all of the explicit order within creation.

So if the Father is the Source and the Logos is the agent of creation in this analogy, what about the Spirit? The Spirit is the unfolding or outgoing wave, the action of God in the world unfolding the pattern of God in and through our lives. The Spirit is the activity of unfolding, like the light shining on the hologram or the receiver unfolding the radio wave. The implicate order of Love that is the Source of creation has been enfolded in creation by the Logos of Love. That order of

---

[55] David Bohm, *The Essential David Bohm*, ed. Lee Nichols (London: Routledge, 2003), 80.

[56] Bohm, "Hidden Variables and the Implicate Order," 122.

[57] Bohm, *The Essential David Bohm*, 139.

Love is now unfolded into the world in and through the power and activity of the Spirit. The incarnate Word is the preeminent example of what it means to be the enfolded implicate order revealed in the world. The Spirit in Jesus' life exemplifies the unfolding of that enfolded implicate order of Love. How that order unfolds is limited by the context into which it is enfolded. Thus the unfolding also depends on human freedom, and human freedom can be further limited by historical and social context.

Drawing on Karl Rahner's understanding of grace as the self-communication of God through the indwelling of the Holy Spirit, one can draw out a beautiful analogous correlation here between the whole as present in and unfolding itself in all of the parts or subwholes in a way that does not eliminate the independence of the subwholes, but rather is the very ground of their freedom and independence. At the same time, this implicate order or this enfolded wholeness of Love is what creates the interconnection among us. While each of us contains the whole, we each do so in a limited way, but that limitation does not negate the fact that the enfolding of the whole within us is not superficial or secondary, but rather that which is most essential to our existence.

The Spirit is what unites us to one another. In the Spirit we become church. Robert Russell offers a theological reflection on Bohm's image of "wholeness as a theological model for the church":

> Many perceive the church as both the visible body of believers and the invisible body of Christ, reflecting a community whole which cannot be simply equated with those assembled in one place or time. We are called to be members of one body through the mystery of the uniting Spirit, though without losing our individuality and uniqueness. The wholeness of this body supports the wholeness of each part of the body, a theme found in Tillich's dialectic of individualization and participation, in Friedrich Schleiermacher's view that "sin is in each the work of all, and in all the work of each," in Paul's theology of the church as Christ's Body, and in the cosmic scope of Teilhard's vision. In many ways we affirm the reality of the whole body as complementary to each individual person. This forms a striking analogy with the quantum potential in quantum formalism as stressed by Bohm, and in the factorization of the whole into

> relatively autonomous subwholes in the explicate order as Bohm has more recently emphasized.[58]

We are only "catholic" when we recognize that we do not exist as individuals apart from our interrelatedness to the wholeness of God as Love and the wholeness of the Body to which we are knit in and through that love. Unfortunately, we often live lives of individuality, fragmentation, and division rather than the interrelatedness and wholeness that is at the core of our being.

Fragmentation as Our Original Sin

For Bohm, the result of the mechanistic worldview that informs our lives is fragmentation. Fragmentation means that a part is understood as a fragment rather than a subwhole, and divisions are seen as absolute.[59] This fragmentation might be theologically understood as connected to humanity's original sin. Rather than living out our connectedness and wholeness, we live lives of fragmentation, understanding ourselves to be autonomous individuals in a way that engenders separation and division. Bohm concludes, "Fragmentary thinking is giving rise to a reality that is constantly breaking up into disorderly, disharmonious, and destructive partial activities" and suggests that a way of thinking that starts with the whole might "bring about a different reality, one that was orderly, harmonious, and creative. But for this to actually happen, it is not enough that we explore this notion only intellectually. It must also enter deeply into our intention, actions, and indeed, into our whole being. That is to say, we have to *mean* it, with all that we think, feel, and do."[60] Our original sin is that rather than enfolded wholeness and love, we have enfolded an implicit sense of division, fragmentation, and prejudice against the other.

One contemporary issue in which we see this fragmentation and division play out is in the relationship between our judicial and criminal justice system and persons of color. If a police officer has been raised

---

[58] Russell, "The Physics of David Bohm and Its Relevance to Philosophy and Theology," 155.

[59] Bohm, "The Implicate Order," 35–36.

[60] Ibid., 37.

in a society that internalizes certain implicit biases (for example, persons of color, particularly males, are larger, stronger, more dangerous than their white counterparts), even though these biases have no basis in reality and the officer may not have any explicit thoughts of prejudice—in fact the officer may *be* a person of color—the officer's actions will flow from the implicit meaning he or she unconsciously attributes to the situation.[61] The officer's biological response will be different based on these implicit meanings, and two similar situations can unfold very differently depending on the person's race without the officer ever being consciously aware that he or she would respond differently if the person in question were not a person of color.

Bohm offers an explanation for the way in which these implicit biases become the tragic actions we see in the headlines of the newspaper. He describes the relationship among language, thought, feelings, intentions, and will, where each in its turn enfolds and unfolds the others. All of these unfold into action. He states: "The thought of danger unfolds into a feeling of fear, which further unfolds into words communicating the feeling, and into thoughts aimed at obtaining security. Likewise, thoughts and feelings together enfold intentions. These are in turn sharpened into a determinate will, and the urge to do something. Thus intention, will, and urge unfold into action, which includes more thought, if necessary."[62] He notes that meaning is always more implicit than what is made explicit in thought and language, and this implicit meaning can result in intention and action.[63] Thus we can act in ways that go beyond the meaning we have made explicit. Bohm gives the example similar to the issue in our criminal justice system described above:

---

[61] See Chris Mooney, "The Science of Why Cops Shoot Young Black Men," *Mother Jones* (December 1, 2014). See also Phillip Goff et al., "The Essence of Innocence: Consequences of Dehumanizing Black Children," *Journal of Personality and Social Psychology* 106, no. 4 (2014): 526–45; Adam Waytz, Kelly Marie Hoffman, and Sophie Trawalter, "A Superhumanization Bias in Whites' Perceptions of Blacks," *Social Psychological and Personality Science* 6, no. 3 (April 1, 2015): 352–59; Catherine A. Cottrell and Steven L. Neuberg, "Different Emotional Reactions to Different Groups: A Sociofunctional Threat-Based Approach to 'Prejudice,'" *Journal of Personality and Social Psychology* 88, no. 5 (2005): 770–89.

[62] Bohm, "The Implicate Order," 29.

[63] Bohm, "Hidden Variables and the Implicate Order," 122–23.

> If a form seen in the dark means "an assailant," the adrenalin flows, the heart beats faster, and one's intention will probably be to run, fight, or freeze. But if, after a second look, it means "only a shadow," the state of the body and the nervous system will be totally different, from which will unfold very different intentions and actions. So what something means to us is intrinsic to what we are, in the sense that our entire physical and mental state, along with our actions, will be profoundly affected by it. Moreover, through meaning what we are is internally related to greater wholes (e.g., to society, which provides a vast general background of such meanings, that we pick up from early childhood on).[64]

The implicit biases that a police officer might carry, in which a person of color is viewed as stronger, bigger, and more dangerous than a white person, unfolds in thoughts, feelings, intentions, and ultimately action. If an officer carries such implicit biases, and the research shows that we all do carry such biases, the officer's actual physical and biochemical reaction to the situation may be different when encountering a person of color, involving an increase in adrenalin and the fight response.[65] Without addressing the implicit biases that are a result of fragmentation and racism in our society, we will not be able to redress the injustice and abuse that occurs within our criminal justice system. So long as we insist on seeing the death of a person of color at the hands of a law enforcement officer as an aberrant occurrence that results from the external interactions of two individuals, rather than seeing those two individuals as interconnected to a greater whole, we will not be able to address the deeper issue of fragmentation and systemic bias that has embedded itself in our society as a whole.

David Bohm notes that our language itself reinforces the notion of fragmentation rather than wholeness. He explains that the subject-verb-object structure of our grammar "implies that all action arises in a separate entity, the subject, and that, in cases described by a

---

[64] Ibid., 123.

[65] Mahzarin R. Banaji, *Blindspot: Hidden Biases of Good People*, ed. Anthony G. Greenwald (New York: Delacorte Press, 2013); "State of the Science: Implicit Bias Review 2015," Kirwan Institute for the Study of Race and Ethnicity, The Ohio State University, online.

transitive verb, this action crosses over the space between them to another separate entity, the object."[66] In other words, our language is structured in such a way as to reinforce our understanding of ourselves as separate individuals rather than reinforcing the ways in which we are interconnected.

This false fragmentation is particularly important in the way it distorts our understanding of God. God is understood as another individual alongside us who acts in the world as we do, albeit on a grander scale. For example, to say that God loves or God loves us implies a false distinction between God and Love. One might say, "Love loves." Likewise, when this same grammatical structure of our language is applied to the Trinity, we end up talking about the Three as three individuals. The Trinity is not three subjects who relate to one another, but rather God is relation or relating. God is verb rather than noun, and yet we also say that God is personal subject, so we think of God as a noun. As Paul Knitter puts is, "For God, 'to be' is nothing other than 'to relate.'"[67] Relation is what is primary in the Trinity. What we call Persons in the Trinity are nothing other than the unfolding of the relations or relatedness that the Trinity is. Love is a particularly appropriate title for God because it can function as both subject and verb. One can address God as Love, and the title is both personal and descriptive.

Bohm shows this peculiar nature of the way we speak with the example "it is raining." What is the "it" that is doing the raining? he asks. He suggests it would be more appropriate to say, "Rain is going on."[68] Bohm suggests that we could resolve this issue by giving the basic role to the verb rather than the noun and thus "help to end the sort of fragmentation indicated above, for the verb describes actions and movements, which flow into each other and merge, without sharp separations or breaks."[69] Fascinatingly, he remarks that ancient Hebrew did take the verb as primary, and so the root of most words

[66] Bohm, *Wholeness and the Implicate Order*, 36. He explains that when the verb is intransitive, the activity of the verb is understood to be a property or reflexive action of the subject, for example, "he moves" means "he moves *himself*" (ibid.).

[67] Paul F. Knitter, *Without Buddha I Could Not Be a Christian* (Oxford: Oneworld, 2009), 19.

[68] Bohm, *Wholeness and the Implicate Order*, 37.

[69] Ibid.

in ancient Hebrew is a verbal form.[70] Hence, the name for God in Hebrew, YHWH, is in essence the verb for "to be." God is a verb, not a noun in Hebrew, even though that verb is taken as a personal name and therefore a subject.

As we let the wholeness of reality, and in our religious perspective, the Trinity, permeate our being and inform our thinking, it can change our actions. Doing so means shining a light on our biases to make them explicit so that we are not acting out of our implicit acceptance of fragmentation. Bohm points out that the word *religion*

> is either from the Latin, *religare*, meaning "to bind together," or from *relegere*, meaning "to gather together." . . . It is also relevant here to consider the word *holy*, whose root meaning is "whole" along with the word *heal* which means "to make whole." All of this indicates that religion is concerned primarily with the *wholeness of life*, as well as of the universe, of humanity, of the individual, and so on.[71]

Bohm goes on to note the irony that while religion intends to make whole, it often does so in terms of absolutes, and therefore, in the end, causes even more division and fragmentation.[72] Likewise, when we think of catholicity as the wholeness of love, too often the Roman Catholic Church has been experienced as a source of fragmentation rather than wholeness. Part of the call of those baptized Christian is to restore the wholeness of the fragmented church, a wholeness that goes beyond any particular denomination or even Christianity itself to embrace all of creation.

In Bohm's discussion of fragmentation, he notes that while religion and science have both contributed to this fragmentation, the main culprit is the human ego.[73] He states:

> Something much more powerful and pervasive is the identification of self or ego as absolutely separate and distinct from

---

[70] Ibid.

[71] Bohm, "Fragmentation and Wholeness in Religion and in Science," 125.

[72] Ibid., 126.

[73] Ibid.

> others. What is relevant here is not only the individual ego, but also the collective ego in the form of family, profession, nation, political or religious ideology, and so on. Fundamentally, all human conflicts arise in the attempt to protect such ego interests, which are generally regarded as supreme, over-riding everything else, and not open to discussion or rational criticism.[74]

Bohm raises the questions: "Why is the ego, individual or collective, so important? Why must it be considered to be essentially perfect and always right? Why do people explode into violence and anger when they are insulted personally, or even more, when family, religion, nation, or ideology are treated in what they regard as an outrageous way?"[75] Without claiming affiliation with the Judeo-Christian tradition, Bohm hearkens back to the theological revelation of Moses and the naming of God as "I am" or "I am who am." He suggests that what is relevant about this revelation is that nothing is predicated of "I am," and where religion goes astray is in adding predicates to the universal "I am," which immediately places limitations on what is unlimited.[76] He goes on to argue that when human persons assume the universal "I am" for themselves and then predicate something ("I am X"), they end up attributing universal significance to something that is limited and partial.[77] In other words, they create an idol. Bohm suggests that part of the solution to this egotism of humanity might be for those of religious belief to understand the "I am" as this "universal energy pervaded with intelligence and love, which is the ground of everything" and that if it is in fact "possible for a human being (or a group of human beings) actually to come into contact with this energy and perhaps even to be aware of himself (or themselves) as a manifestation of it," the problem of the ego will be dissolved.[78] Our God as Triune Love calls us to bring catholicity, the wholeness of that love, to birth in the world.

Bohm describes an order he calls "generative order." The unfolding of the implicate order is due to the generative order but also to

---

[74] Ibid., 130.
[75] Ibid., 131.
[76] Ibid., 132.
[77] Ibid.
[78] Ibid., 133.

"the constraints of that upon which the order works."[79] For Bohm, the implicate order is generative in that it generates wholly new forms or new patterns, and the whole is enfolded in each new pattern.[80] The new forms or new patterns are created because the whole unfolds in each subwhole, but it does so within the unique context of that particular subwhole and so generates something new each time. Similarly we can say that the Trinity is enfolded in each of our lives, but the form or pattern is different and unique in each one of us due to the constraints of finite being, to our particular context, and to our personal freedom to say yes or no, to participate or not, in the unfolding of wholeness. Part of the constraints of finite being is the fact that finite being exists in a socio-historical context, so not only is the pattern constrained by time, space, and materiality, not only is it constrained by our own freedom and choices, but it is also constrained by the social context into which we are born and in which we live—our race, gender, class, nationality, and so on. All of us are created in the image and likeness of the Triune God, but how that pattern then unfolds in our individual lives is unique.

The Holy Spirit unfolding the new and unique pattern in each of our lives is the generative order. The Spirit is the giver of life. While that pattern is constrained by the circumstances of our individual lives and socio-historical context, each pattern has the potential to change the whole pattern as it is unfolded in creation. That is not to say that we have the potential to change the whole that is God, but rather that we have the potential to participate in how that pattern of the whole that is God unfolds in the created world. We co-create the catholicity of the world.

Lee Smolin's Loop Quantum Gravity and Perichoresis

While David Bohm's hidden variables explanation of quantum physics is not a widely accepted theory among physicists, the idea that relationality is at the core of the cosmos and all that exists is found in some of the ground-breaking theories of the present day. Lee Smolin is a theoretical physicist specializing in loop quantum gravity, another

[79] David Bohm, "Dialogue on Science, Society, and the Generative Order," *Zygon* 25, no. 4 (1990): 450.

[80] Ibid.

theory attempting to reconcile relativity and quantum mechanics. Smolin proposes theories of understanding reality that begin with the relationality of all that exists. When one believes in a Trinity that is relation, Smolin's view of a physical world that reflects that relationality offers a congruent vision of the created world.

Like Bohm, Smolin is drawn to a hidden variables understanding of quantum physics as well, believing that "there is an objective physical reality and that something describable happens as an electron jumps from one energy level of an atom into another."[81] However, his objection to the Bohm–de Broglie theory is that it is not reciprocal, in that the wave influences the particle, but the particle does not influence the wave.[82] Smolin suggests an alternative model built off of the ensemble model, which looks not at a single electron, but rather the collection of similar atoms.[83] His model begins with interrelatedness.

The popular block spacetime model that emerged from Einstein's theory of relativity views time as sort of an illusion of human experience, proposing that all time already exists as simply another dimension in the same way that all space exists. Smolin proposes an alternative view in which time is fundamentally real, and space is an emergent property.[84] While the models he uses to explain this possibility are still theoretical, he notes that "they show that if everything is potentially connected to everything else, then there must be a global time. The relativity of simultaneity in special relativity is a consequence of locality."[85] In its birth or creation our universe was nonlocal. As space emerged, those nonlocal connections get switched off, and locality emerges. Thus, while our relationships are local, in that we don't experience our connectedness to all that exists or in Bohm's terms the implicate order enfolded within us, at our core is nonlocality, our interconnection with everything or in Bohm's words the enfolded implicate order.

---

[81] Lee Smolin, *Time Reborn: From the Crisis in Physics to the Future of the Universe* (Boston: Houghton Mifflin Harcourt, 2013), 157.

[82] Ibid., 159.

[83] Ibid., 159, 160–61. The theory that inspired Smolin uses a hypothetical collection of atoms, but Smolin suggests that one can use the actual collection of real atoms throughout the universe through nonlocal connections.

[84] Ibid. See also 57–58, 164–66, 171.

[85] Ibid., 159, 191.

In the Christian tradition we talk about the image and likeness of God that are unfolded within us through the process of theosis or divinization. The Christian tradition has a word it uses for an interrelatedness that allows for the continued distinctiveness and uniqueness of that which is related. That word is *perichoresis,* a Greek word that means "to encompass one another"; it is often described as mutual interpenetration. It is a word that is difficult to translate, but it is intended to indicate absolute interrelatedness that preserves distinction or uniqueness. Within the patristic tradition we talk about the perichoresis of the human and divine nature in Christ, the perichoresis of the Three within the Trinity, and in Maximus the Confessor a perichoresis in creation itself that mirrors the perichoresis of the Trinity. Lee Smolin gives us a scientific vision of creation that can be connected to this idea of perichoresis, the idea that each aspect of creation finds its uniqueness and distinction in its interrelatedness. In other words, we find our uniqueness in our catholicity, in our relatedness to the wholeness of love.

In his theory of loop quantum gravity Smolin suggests that relationship is the key to reality. He argues that space itself is nothing more (or less) than the relationship among objects.[86] Smolin uses the example of a sentence to explain. A sentence is nothing more (or less) that the relationship among words. A list of words in itself is not a sentence. Reality is a network of relationships among objects or, more accurately, events. Time is the way we measure change in that network of relationships.[87] So, in this scientific theory the core of reality mirrors what we are proclaiming to be the essence of the God who created that reality (note that Smolin himself does not propose or accept the idea of God/Creator). God/Love who is relation creates a world that is also relation. Space and time, rather than being the framework of reality, emerge from those relationships that constitute reality.

Objects, in Smolin's theory, are not things but rather events or processes.[88] Human beings are not objects or even subjects but rather stories.[89] Those stories reveal who we are as persons. He goes on

---

[86] Lee Smolin, *Three Roads to Quantum Gravity* (New York: Basic Books, 2001), 18–19.

[87] Ibid., 22.

[88] Ibid., 49.

[89] Ibid., 49–50.

to explain that the difference between a story and a list of events is causality, the connections among the events.[90] The difference is like that between a sentence and a list of words. The former in both cases involves connections. The only difference between these stories/processes and what we call objects is the speed at which change occurs.[91] All objects (for example, a rock) change as well, but the speed of change is on a monumentally different scale than what we experience in our lives. Smolin states that the idea that the world is composed of objects is an illusion:

> If this were really the way the world is, then the primary description of something would be how it is, and change in it would be secondary. Change would be nothing but alterations in how something is. But relativity and quantum theory each tell us that this is not how the world is. They tell us—no better, they scream at us—that our world is a history of processes. Motion and change are primary. Nothing *is*, except in a very approximate and temporary sense. How something is, or what its state is, is an illusion. . . . "Is" is an illusion. So to speak the language of the new physics we must learn a vocabulary in which process is more important than, and prior to, stasis.[92]

So why is this point important to our thinking about Trinity? For two reasons: First, because in the world we know and experience, becoming takes precedence over being. God has always been imaged as pure Being, the ground of being. Many philosophers and theologians, however, see God as beyond even being and nonbeing, the ground of both. Our God is the ground not only, or perhaps even primarily, of being but of becoming. In Smolin's world there is no such thing as static being. There is only being that is becoming, existence in which change is primary. Second, Smolin explains that "the universe of events is a *relational universe*. That is, all its properties are described in terms of relationships between the events. The most important relationship that two events can have is *causality*."[93] Thus, in Smolin's view, "time and change are not optional, for the universe

[90] Ibid., 50–51.
[91] Ibid., 52.
[92] Ibid., 53.
[93] Ibid.

is a story, and it is composed of processes."[94] Unlike many physicists, Smolin argues that the most fundamental reality of the cosmos is not space. It is time. Relationships are not static. They evolve in time.

So while we posit eternal relations among the Three of the Trinity, our human relationships cannot be modeled on the Trinity because our relationships, including our relationship to the Triune God, are always evolving and unfolding. The Trinity is Bohm's whole, Bohm's implicate order, grounded in the monarchy of the Father, not as ruler in a hierarchical sense, but as source. That implicate order enfolded into creation by the Logos and revealed in the incarnate Word that is Jesus of Nazareth is then unfolded in time as story. The unfolding does not happen all at once. It happens in and through these processes, in and through the story that is the cosmos.

When we think about the infinity of the Triune God, we can realize that humans may be but a small chapter of that unfolding story in an evolving cosmos that may be part of a multiverse and may be both the result and the cause of other universes. We need not be threatened by that idea when we think about implicate order, because even though we are only "part" of the story, we are also the "whole" story. Our relationship with the Triune God is no less whole because the context of our unfolding that relationship in the story of the cosmos is limited.

Relationality, then, can also be seen as an implicate order of God as Love and Source of all that is. Relationality is part of wholeness. We can say that catholicity is relationality that is grounded in the oneness or wholeness of God as Love. Here we have that doctrine of the Trinity, in that the relationality of the Three creates the oneness of the whole, and the oneness of the whole grounds the relationality of the Three. Love is the Source of the relationality, both in the Trinity and in creation. That Love as Word reveals itself in relationality, both in the Trinity and in the relatedness inherent in creation itself. That Love as Spirit acts—loves, if you will—in the power and dynamism of relationality both in the Trinity and in and through the relatedness of creation. To use Bohm's model again, one could say that there is an implicate order of relationality. That relationality is enfolded into creation by the Logos. Relationality is the order or plan of creation itself. Relationality is the super-implicate and generative order of creation. That relationality is then unfolded in creation in and through the unfolding of relationships that create space and time. On a human

[94] Ibid.

level that relationality is what makes us human persons, and our being persons in relation is revealed to us in the incarnate Christ and enacted in the Spirit that binds us together as church, as the body of Christ.

Here one also reencounters the threefold notion of perichoresis in the Trinity, in the incarnate Christ, and in creation itself, as a way of understanding what it means for relatedness or relationality to be at the center of reality. First, perichoresis describes the complete interpenetration of the Three in the Trinity in a way that creates/preserves the distinction and uniqueness of each. Like Bohm's concept of wholes and subwholes, each of the Three is a whole and yet each of the Three contains the others, who in themselves are also whole, and the Three as One are the Whole. Such an image can be connected back to Athanasius's understanding of *consubstantial,* which we explore more deeply in Chapter 4. Denis Edwards says that for Athanasius, "God cannot be divided into parts, but the Son is whole from whole as eternal Image and Radiance of the Father."[95] Athanasius underscores the centrality of relationality in the Trinity. The interrelatedness of the Three is what defines each (the Son is the Son of the Father, and the Father is the Father of the Son, or to use my terminology, Love is the Source of the Word of Love Revealed, and the Word of Love reveals the Source of Love) and what unites each. Perichoresis is used to explain the relations of the Three within the Trinity, each mutually interpenetrating the others in a way that both creates and preserves the distinction of each.

Second, in the perichoresis of the human and divine natures of Christ, Christ is fully human because his human nature is perfectly fulfilled, interpenetrated with, the divine, without thereby making it anything other than human—fully and perfectly human. The divine is revealed in the humanity. The humanity of Jesus is the expression of the divine love in the world. In Christ, humanity and creation as a whole are brought into and encompassed by the divine.

Finally, perichoresis is used to refer to the interconnectedness of creation itself in the tradition of Maximus the Confessor. The interconnectedness of reality that physicists like David Bohm and Lee Smolin investigate on a scientific level can be understood from a theological perspective as the result of creation reflecting the Creator.

---

[95] Denis Edwards, "Athanasius' Letters to Serapion: Resource for a Twenty-First-Century Theology of God the Trinity," *Phronema* 29, no. 2 (2014): 45.

God the Source of Love creates through the expression of the Word of Love by the power of the Spirit of Love. The perichoresis of creation is in the image of the perichoresis of the Three in the Trinity. The core of reality itself is interconnection and wholeness. At the heart of all reality is catholicity, the wholeness of love.

Chapter 2

From Being to Love

In recent decades trinitarian theology has experienced a resurgence of popularity in theological thought. A large part of this resurgence has taken place in discussions devoted to a theology of the social Trinity. As Karen Kilby states, "The chief strategy used to revivify the doctrine and establish its relevance has come to be the advocacy of a *social* understanding of the Trinity."[1] Stanley Grenz would concur, noting that "by the end of the twentieth century, the concept of relationality had indeed moved to center stage. In fact the assumption that the most promising beginning point for a viable Trinitarian theology lies in the constellation of relationships between the three persons had become so widely accepted that it attained a kind of quasi-orthodox status."[2] As we saw in Chapter 1, relationality is at the core of reality itself. Any trinitarian theology should begin with the concept of relationality.

---

[1] Karen Kilby, "Perichoresis and Projection: Problems with Social Doctrines of the Trinity," *New Blackfriars* 81 (2001): 432. Kilby highlights Jürgen Moltmann's work *The Trinity and the Kingdom of God* as the beginning of this movement (432–33). Among her designation of those who are social trinitarians, she also includes Leonardo Boff and John Zizioulas (344n3). The primary focus of the article, however, is on Jürgen Moltmann and Colin Gunton.

[2] Stanley Grenz, *Rediscovering the Triune God: The Trinity in Contemporary Theology* (Minneapolis: Fortress Press, 2004), 117–18. In the chapter titled "The Triumph of Relationality," Grenz presents the work of Leonardo Boff and Catherine Mowry LaCugna, among others.

The problem with these schools of thought promoting a social trinitarianism or a social analogy of the Trinity is the danger of it being misconceived in a tritheistic manner.[3] Part of the issue is the manner in which these social trinitarians use the word *Person* in combination with the concept of community. Veli-Matti Kärkkäinen notes: "One frequent question to [Jürgen] Moltmann and other social trinitarians is whether they have ended up affirming tritheism in their fear of 'monotheism.' Scholars from a wide variety of orientations have expressed strong concerns about tritheism; some even leveled the charge of tritheism."[4] While we will engage the thought of the social trinitarians in more depth in Chapter 6, this chapter examines the concept of person and suggests that there is a need today to find new analogies to balance the overemphasis that has been placed on the language of person.

One model for making such a shift can be found in the work of Jean-Luc Marion, who shifts from Being to Love as the primary analogue for God. We can build on Marion's analogical shift by proposing a similar shift from person to Love in trinitarian imagery. Traditional theology from Augustine to Aquinas to Rahner has conceived of God as Being. Jean-Luc Marion contends that our only hope for avoiding idolatry is to praise God as Love as opposed to conceiving of God as Being. The shift away from an understanding of God as Being has implications for trinitarian theology as well. How do we speak of Trinity in light of this shift in analogical focus? I would suggest the trinitarian analogy of the Unoriginate Source of Love revealed in the Word and enacted in the Spirit. Thus we can see what it means to be person, not by looking to the Three Persons of the Trinity, but in God united to humanity in the incarnation, in the *person* of Jesus the Christ. We can see what it means to be community, not in the relations among the three Persons of the Trinity, but in God united to humanity in the Spirit-filled Christian community described in scripture.[5] By using love as the primary analogue, one can conceive

---

[3] See Veli-Matti Kärkkäinen, *The Trinity: Global Perspectives* (Louisville, KY: Westminster John Knox Press, 2007), 115–22, particularly notes 122 and 123 on Moltmann, and 286–91, particularly note 99 on Boff.

[4] Ibid., 115nn122–23.

[5] The early Spirit-filled community is described in Acts and the Letters, for example, Acts 2:42–47 and Acts 4:32–35, which emphasize an egalitarian community that shares resources equally among its members.

of God as personal rather than as person, as relational rather than as being, while simultaneously avoiding the idea that God is *a* being or *a* subject—in short, while avoiding anthropomorphizing God, which is to say, turning God into a big human in the sky.

One challenge addressed through this alternative model is the need for a concept of person as relational as opposed to the modern understanding of the person as individual. Rather than turning to the Three of the Trinity for a model of what it means to be a person, we turn to Jesus Christ, the incarnation of God as Love in union with humanity, as the one who reveals what it means to be person. As corollaries to this challenge are the need for an emphasis on community and equality and a concern that the Trinity be a doctrine that functions as a catalyst for social change, combating oppression and fighting for social justice in the world. The model for community or what it means to be in communion need not be located in the relationships among the Three of the Trinity. Rather, the model can be found in the Holy Spirit creating the body of Christ as exemplified in the witness of scripture.[6]

The Word *Person* in Trinitarian Theology

As Ángel Cordovilla Pérez explains, the Latin word *persona* and the Greek word *prosopon* have a complicated history:

> The Latin term signified a variety of things: role or character in theatre (Plautus, Terence); the person of the verb in grammar (Varro); or individual in a social sense (Cicero). The Greek term *prosopon* is already witnessed to in Homer with the meaning of 'face', comes to mean 'to gaze', then 'that which is seen', and will finish tied into the world of theatre in the Hellenistic period. Finally, the meaning of *hypostasis* is determined by its etymology. Composed of *hypo-* (under) and the root *sta* (to hold

[6] For an excellent ecclesiological description of the relationship of the Trinity to the church as body of Christ, albeit one that depends on a social analogy of the Trinity through Zizioulas and Volf, see Marcel Sarot, "Trinity and Church: Trinitarian Perspectives on the Identity of the Christian Community," *International Journal of Systematic Theology* 12 (2010): 33–45.

> oneself), it originally had a common meaning of foundation, base, cement or point of departure for an expedition.[7]

The word *person* today has taken on a meaning correlative to the word *human*, picking up along the way both Boethius's definition of a rational individual and Descartes's contribution of consciousness and cognition (I think, therefore I am). Karl Rahner notes "the danger of a popular, unverbalized, but at bottom quite massive tritheism" inherent in the word *Person*.[8] He suggests that "speaking of three persons in God entails almost inevitably the danger . . . of believing that there exist in God three distinct consciousnesses, spiritual vitalities, centers of activity, and so on."[9] Noting all the caveats we have to put on our use of this terminology, he muses:

> But honesty finally forces us to inquire, not without misgivings, why we still call "persons" that which remains ultimately of God's threefold "personality," since we have to remove from these persons precisely that which at first we thought of as constituting a person. Later on, when the more subtle remarks of the theologians have been forgotten, we see that once more we glide probably into a false and basically tritheistic conception, as we think of the three persons as of three different personalities with different centers of activity.[10]

Rahner argues that the word *person* nonetheless holds pride of place in our tradition and cannot be abandoned, but he recognizes that at times it may be necessary to use a different term. He explains:

> It is true, of course, that theology may theoretically keep such modifications of meaning away from *its* concept of person, by

[7] Ángel Cordovilla Pérez, "The Trinitarian Concept of Person," in *Rethinking Trinitarian Theology: Disputed Questions and Contemporary Issues in Trinitarian Theology*, ed. Giulio Maspero and Robert J. Wozniak (London: T & T Clark, 2012), 109.

[8] Karl Rahner, *The Trinity*, trans. Joseph Donceel (New York: Crossroad Publishing, 1997), 42.

[9] Ibid., 43.

[10] Ibid.

> clearly formulated "definitions." But in fact the Church is not the mistress and guide of such a history of concepts. Thus in principle it is not apriorily impossible that the word may develop historically in such a way that, at long last, despite the theoretical right of the magisterium to "regulate the language of the community," a right which is included in every dogmatic decision, it may be impossible to use the word in the kerygma without incurring the danger of tritheistic misunderstanding.[11]

In other words, theologians and the magisterium of the Catholic Church can put all sorts of caveats on how we are using the word *person*, explaining that we do not mean what the word means in our everyday language. In the end, however, those caveats are not going to be front and center in people's minds when they hear the word applied to the Trinity. Instead, most people will hear the word in the way that it is used in our everyday language and thus conceive of the Trinity as three individuals, each with its own center of cognition, consciousness, and will. In a word, they will unknowingly be tritheists.

The evolution of this word *person* caused theologians such as Barth and Rahner to suggest alternatives such as "mode of being" or "mode of subsistence" when discussing trinitarian theology.[12] Rahner explains that "when we say: 'there are three persons in God, God subsists in three persons' we generalize and add up something which cannot be added up, since that which alone is really common to Father, Son, and Spirit is precisely the one and only Godhead, and since there is no higher point of view from which the three can be added *as* Father, Son, and Spirit."[13] In other words, as a sweatshirt I owned as a grad student stated, MARQUETTE THEOLOGY DEPARTMENT—THE ONLY DEPARTMENT ON CAMPUS WHERE 1+1+1=1. When we add up three human persons, we have three because we are adding up three individuals. When we use *person* in regard to the Trinity, we are trying to articulate distinction without individuality. Rahner adds that "we never discover in our experience a case where what 'subsists as distinct'

[11] Ibid., 57.

[12] Ibid., 124. See John Gresham, "The Social Model of the Trinity and Its Critics," *Scottish Journal of Theology* 46 (1993): 328–31.

[13] Rahner, *The Trinity*, 104.

can be thought of as multiplied without a multiplication of natures."[14] We cannot think of something being distinct that is not also its own individual thing. Rahner also points out that adding to the confusion is the fact that theology uses the word *person* differently in trinitarian theology, as that which distinguishes the trinitarian Persons, than it does in Christology, as that which unites the two natures of Christ.[15]

The concerns of those who favor using the word *person* are that we cannot eliminate a word that is such a foundation of our traditional trinitarian theology and that the alternative phrases suggested do not capture the personal nature of God as revealed in scripture. The social trinitarians argue that the word *person* as it is nuanced and redefined to apply to the Trinity can be taken to be a corrective to our individualistic understanding of *person* as it is used to describe a human being. Admittedly, the word *person* cannot be entirely abandoned in trinitarian theology, as it does hold a place of preeminence in our dogma and is used in the writings of the ecumenical councils. However, the word, with all the meanings it has accrued over time, has become an idol, to use Jean-Luc Marion's term, and thus must be counterbalanced with new images. Recognizing that all of our language about God is ultimately analogy and metaphor, when one image starts to be used exclusively and literally, it is in danger of becoming idolatrous.[16] The point that Elizabeth Johnson makes in regard to the use of male-dominant language for God can also be true of the word *Person* in trinitarian language: it is idolatrous "insofar as [it] is honored as the only or the supremely fitting way of speaking about God, it absolutizes a single set of metaphors and obscures the height and depth and length and breadth of divine mystery. Thus it does damage to the very truth of God that theology is supposed to cherish and promote."[17] Thus, we should not eliminate the word *Person* altogether from our trinitarian language, but we do need to counter that imagery with words such as *Love* to balance the dangerous tendency toward literalism that arises when any one image is used exclusively.

---

[14] Ibid., 105.

[15] Ibid.

[16] See Elizabeth Johnson, *She Who Is: The Mystery of God in Feminist Theological Discourse* (New York: Crossroad, 1992), 33–34.

[17] Ibid., 18.

In terms of the second and third points in favor of using the word *Person*, that it is more personal and can be a corrective to the secular usage of the word, Love as an analogy for God does address the personal nature of God because Love is by definition personal and relational. The social trinitarians particularly emphasize this third point that the word *Person* as used in trinitarian theology offers a corrective to the individualistic interpretation of the word as applied to the human being. However, more often the tendency is to apply the individualistic interpretation to God rather than the communal interpretation to the human person.[18] In other words, rather than being a way of showing humans how to be more Godlike, using the social analogy encourages us to think of God as more humanlike. The way the social analogy uses the word *person* gives rise to an image of God as three human persons sitting around a table "relating" to one another in a small community. Picture, if you will, the famous Rublev icon of the Trinity as the three visitors to Abraham literally sitting around a table. Despite Rublev's attempts to avoid a tritheistic conception by giving each Person the same face, one walks away with an image of three individual people.

Jean-Luc Marion's *God without Being*

Jean-Luc Marion offers a radical approach in rethinking the concept of God: to leave behind the image of God as Being altogether. He suggests that rather than thinking of God primarily in terms of Being, the primary (though not exclusive) analogy for God must be love, agape, gift. In the preface to the English edition of his seminal work, *God without Being*, Marion asks, "Does Being define the first and highest of divine names? . . . No doubt, God can and must in the end also be; but does his relation to Being determine him as radically as the relation to his Being defines all other beings?"[19] He is not saying that God does

---

[18] For an excellent argument against using the Trinity to understand human persons, see Kathryn Tanner, "Social Trinitarianism and Its Critics," in Maspero and Wozniak, *Rethinking Trinitarian Theology*, 368–86, particularly 378–80.

[19] Jean-Luc Marion, *God without Being: Hors-Texte*, trans. Thomas A. Carlson, 2nd edition (Chicago: University of Chicago Press, 2012), xxii.

not exist, but rather asks whether being determines God. As noted in the section on Maximus the Confessor, Being determines us; it does not determine God. God is beyond both being and nonbeing.

Marion begins his work by marking various contrasts: idol versus icon, mirror versus face, concept versus gift. In each of these dichotomies the first term limits and constrains the infinite, rebounding our gaze back upon ourselves. Marion describes the idol as "the low water mark of the divine" or "what the human gaze has experienced of the divine."[20] The idol is not bad in and of itself. Rather, Marion is addressing our experience of God and the way we tend to articulate that experience: it becomes an idol, an absolute, a limit on the infinity and incomprehensibility of God. Using our experience as a way to talk about God is not bad, as long as we recognize the limitations of doing so. We must recognize that there is a certain idolatry inherent in applying human experiences, concepts, and words to God who is ultimately beyond any human experience, concept, or word. The idol or concept is problematic not due to failure or illusion, but rather due to "the conditions of its validity—its radical immanence to the one who experiences it, and experiences it, rightly so, as impassible."[21] Marion is saying because these images come from our experience of God, we are too close to them. They become very personal, and rightly so, but that very intimate connection to a particular image endows it with a false certainty. We feel that one particular image is right and others are wrong. We begin to feel that the image cannot be changed. The image becomes an idol. It is a mirror, in Marion's terms, because it reflects back to us our own idea of God rather than allowing us to be in a dynamic relationship with the God of mystery who is always revealing new surprises to us. Think of your own human relationships. We tend toward misunderstandings in our relationships with others when we start to presume we know other persons and make assumptions rather than continually allowing them to reveal themselves to us. I remember once hearing a person being interviewed on the radio about raising teenagers. She said that the biggest mistake we can make with our teens as parents is to assume we know who they are. She said she tries to approach each day looking to learn one new thing about her teen in that day. We need to approach our relationship with God in a similar manner that is open to the mystery God is.

---

[20] Ibid., 14.

[21] Ibid., 28.

Marion notes that a concept of God is not an illusion. A concept catches hold of the imagination of a particular age because it expresses the experience of God for that age. We use our words, ideas, and images to think about and relate to God. Due to the concrete nature of a concept or image, however, it very quickly becomes an idol, an image that constrains the infinity and incomprehensibility of God.[22] One thinks of the story of Thomas Aquinas, who wrote the *Summa Theologiae*, a masterpiece of words and concepts about God, who toward the end of his life received a personal revelation of God and then said of his great work that it all seemed like straw to him. Our concepts and images of God are true in what they express of our experience of God, but they will always also be false idols in that no word, concept, or image can adequately express God. Compared to the mystery of God, our words are all like straw.

In light of that insight, we do not need to eliminate the word *person* as a concept from our trinitarian imagery; it is part of a longstanding, creedal, Christian tradition. In order that *person* not become an idol, however, we need to counterbalance this concept with the new icon, face, gift of Love. In contrast to an idol that stops our gaze, Marion suggests the icon as that which opens us to the absolute otherness of God, and thus the visible icon engenders for us an experience of the invisible God. We don't grasp God. In the icon, God grasps us. Rather than our own ideas being reflected back to us, the icon pulls us beyond ourselves, challenging us in new ways.[23] Here one sees the contrast between the idol and the icon or the mirror and the face. The idol or mirror closes; the icon or face opens.[24] The idol reinforces our own thinking; the icon invites us to new ways of thinking. The mirror only allows us to see ourselves; the face is an encounter with the mystery of the other. The icon, as opposed to the idol, allows one to enter into the infinity and

---

[22] Ibid., 30. Marion explains that the concept "exposes what Dasein, at the moment of a particular epoch, experiences of the divine and approves as the definition of its 'God.' Only such an experience of the Divine is not founded so much in God as in man: . . . the concept marks the extreme advance, then the reflected return, of a thought that renounces venturing beyond itself, into the aim of the invisible."

[23] Ibid., 19.

[24] Ibid., 19–20. See also Jean-Luc Marion, *The Erotic Phenomenon*, trans. Stephen E. Lewis (Chicago: University of Chicago Press, 2007), 97–101.

incomprehensibility of God, the place where we cannot grasp God, but rather are grasped by God.

To make a distinction between God who is idol and God who is icon, Marion uses a cross over the letter "o" in God as a visual reminder to us of the limitation of our concepts, a reminder that all words and concepts are, in a sense, idols. Some contemporary Jewish theologians follow the ancient tradition of not saying the name of God by writing G-d to remind us of the sacredness of that name and the holiness of God's mystery. Likewise Marion suggests we "cross out" the word *God* to remind ourselves that the words we use can never capture the reality of God. God is always beyond our words and concepts.

While Marion would argue that the concept of Being has become an idol, he recognizes that to abandon the category of being in reference to God threatens our ability to say anything all. Marion queries, "What name, what concept, and what sign nevertheless yet remain feasible? A single one, no doubt, love, . . . 'God is *agape*' (1 John 4:8)."[25] "Why love?" he goes on to ask. For Marion, love, like God, cannot be constrained, limited, or conditioned.[26] Love can be an *icon* of God, because our experience of affect is an experience of the ineffable, of that which is beyond cognition. Heart knowledge goes beyond words, beyond what can be expressed. Love cannot be externally constrained or limited. It is not subject to one who receives it, but is freely poured out. Marion notes that "Love loves without condition, simply because it loves; he [God] thus loves without limit or restriction. No refusal rebuffs or limits that which, in order to give itself, does not await the least welcome or require the least consideration. . . . As interlocutor of love, man does not first have to pretend to arrange a 'divine abode' for it . . . but purely and simply to accept it; to accept it or, more modestly, not to steal away from it."[27] For Marion love is truly love only if it risks not being loved in return. He explains that love is not subject to being:

> Loving loses nothing from the fact of not being, because it gains nothing from the fact of being. Or better, to love consists sometimes in not being—in not being loved, or at least in

[25] Ibid., 47.

[26] Ibid.

[27] Ibid. See also Marion, *The Erotic Phenomenon*, 71–73.

> accepting being able not to be loved. Nothing, neither being nor nothingness, can limit, hold back, or offend love, from the moment that loving implies, by principle, the risk of not being loved. To love without being loved—this defines *love without being*. The simple formal definition of loving includes its victory over nothing, and thus over death. Love raises from the dead—we must understand this as an analytical proposition.[28]

Marion's position is that love does not require reciprocity. You can love someone who does not love you in return. To love someone is to risk not being loved in return. To love someone also risks loss, and yet, Marion notes that love conquers even death. Love does not die when one's loved one dies. Love is greater than being.

Love is also a suitable analogy for God because it is beyond comprehension. As with God, one does not grasp love but rather is grasped by it. Marion argues:

> As opposed to the concept, that by the very definition of apprehension, gathers up what it comprehends . . . love (even and especially if it ends up causing thought, giving rise—by its excess—to thought) does not pretend to comprehend, since it does not mean at all to take; it postulates its own giving, giving where the giver strictly coincides with the gift, without any restriction, reservation, or mastery. Thus love gives itself only in abandoning itself, ceaselessly transgressing the limits of its own gift, so as to be transplanted outside itself.[29]

Love does not gather up or take, love gives of itself. It is self-diffusive and overflows. Love goes outside and beyond itself.

As with God, Love cannot be captured by words or a concept. And yet Marion notes that we need the concept, because without it, "we literally no longer know what we are saying, and in fact, we say nothing."[30] Thus we cannot abandon words or language or concepts altogether. Love becomes a fitting analogy for God because in both

---

[28] Ibid., 72.

[29] Marion, *God without Being*, 48.

[30] Marion, *The Erotic Phenomenon*, 4. See also Jean-Luc Marion, *Prolegomena to Charity*, trans. Stephen E. Lewis (New York: Fordham University Press, 2002), 71ff.

instances we use language in a way that defies comprehension. As Marion notes of his own attempt to speak of love: "And obviously I will do it badly; I will do this phenomenon ill, but that will do me good—if only because it will make me feel my incapacity to say it, just as it will make me take note of my powerlessness to make it."[31]

Our words are never adequate to our love. As a mother, there are no words that can possibly express the love that I feel for my children. And yet love demands expression. I say the words to my children over and over, even though I know that they cannot possibly comprehend the depth of meaning behind those words. Do not such words describe every undertaking of theology, of God-talk? No concept or word is adequate to describe or define God, and yet our relationship demands expression.

Marion replaces the primacy of Being with Love, the "I am" of Exodus 3:14 with the "God is Love" of 1 John.[32] For Marion, the use of Being as the primary analogy for God comes from our human cognitive bias.[33] We project what is essential to our experience of existence onto the essence of God. Using passages from Romans 4:17 and 1 Corinthians 1:26, however, Marion demonstrates how God is not restricted by being. Being and nonbeing are subject to God. God "calls the nonbeings as if they were beings. The call does not take into consideration the [ontic] difference between nonbeings and beings."[34]

---

[31] Marion, *The Erotic Phenomenon*, 10.

[32] Marion, *God without Being*, 73–75. Note that Marion no longer includes Aquinas among those who perpetuate an onto-theology (though he does include many interpreters of Aquinas in this critique). Marion shifted his own position on Aquinas in part due to critiques made by John Milbank. For Marion's adjusted position, see Jean-Luc Marion, "Saint Thomas d'Aquin Et l'Onto-Théologie," *Revue Thomiste* 95, no. 1 (1995): 31–66. See also "Thomas Aquinas and Onto-Theo-Logy," in *Mystics: Presence and Aporia* (Chicago: University of Chicago Press, 2003), 38–74. This article is also included in the second edition of the English translation of *God without Being*, 199–236. For articles discussing this shift and the dialogue with John Milbank, see Merold Westphal, "The Importance of Overcoming Metaphysics for the Life of Faith," *Modern Theology* 23 (2007): 253–78, and Wayne Hankey, "Theoria Versus Poesis: Neoplatonism and Trinitarian Difference in Aquinas, John Milbank, Jean-Luc Marion, and John Zizioulas," *Modern Theology* 15 (1999): 387–415.

[33] Marion, *God without Being*, 80.

[34] Ibid., 88.

God not only calls being into existence; using 1 Corinthians 1:26–29, Marion points out that God can also annul being so that "that which is can be, for God, as if it were not."[35] God as Love is the God "who gives life to the dead and who calls the nonbeings as beings" (Rom. 4:17).[36] God chooses and calls those to whom the world denies humanity and even existence, namely, the weak, the foolish, the lowly.[37] The world divides the world into beings and nonbeings, somethings and nothings, but God reverses that judgment. First Corinthians 1:28 states, "God chose what is low and despised in the world, things that are not, to reduce to nothing things that are."[38] Existence and personhood are not based on the judgment of the world but rather on the call of God and one's response to that call.[39]

Marion goes on to argue that love is not subject to being. Using human love as an example, he explains that when one loses the person one loves, "the world, which is, does not become more loveable for that reason—on the contrary. And the loved one, who is no longer, does not become less lovable for that reason—on the contrary."[40] According to Marion, "that which is, if it does not receive love, is as if it were not, while that which is not, if love polarizes it, is as if it were."[41] Love calls us into being. He concludes that "there is nothing more reasonable than the insanity of sacrificing all that is (being in its totality) for that which is not (the absent loved one). . . . To give the world which is, empty of love, for that which is not but belongs to the domain of love—there is nothing more reasonable and even advantageous."[42] Thus love is beyond any constraint, condition, or definition by being. Marion refers to love, therefore, as the proper horizon for the events which escape reason and rationality, the horizon of "*love without being.*"[43] He insists that for human beings, to be loved and to love is more essential than to exist, and that primacy

---

[35] Ibid., 89.

[36] Ibid., 86.

[37] Ibid., 92–93.

[38] Marion's translation, "God chose the ignoble things of this world [*agenē, ignobilia* says the Vulgate] and the contemptible things, and also the non-beings, in order to annul the beings (*kai ta mē onta, hina ta onta katargēsē*)," ibid., 89.

[39] Ibid., 95.

[40] Ibid., 136. See also *The Erotic Phenomenon,* 5–6, 193.

[41] Marion, *God without Being*, 136.

[42] Ibid., 136–37.

[43] Marion, *The Erotic Phenomenon*, 6.

of love is what separates human beings from the world of objects or animals or artificial intelligence.[44] Marion highlights love as that which makes us distinctly human, and so one might say that it is what makes us to be created in the image and likeness of God. Hence our relationality is at the center of our personhood.[45]

For Marion, God has revealed Godself as this Love in the cross. God for Marion is not Being but Love, and Love is self-gift as is evidenced in the cross.[46] In Christ, God is revealed ultimately, not in being, but in disappearance, in death, in non-Being, which is the epitome of love and self-gift. In *Prolegomena to Charity*, Marion notes that even the most radical presence of God in the Incarnation ultimately resolves itself in the absence of resurrection and ascension.[47] Once again, Marion argues, Love demonstrates its precedence over Being. Marion maintains that the Incarnation is "translated paradoxically, by non-presence—in short, by the contrary of the completed incarnation."[48] He points to this presence by absence in the story of Emmaus:

> Namely: the recognition of the gift of the presence of God in *this* man, because this man can give himself to the point of abandoning himself like bread is distributed, abandoning himself like bread, like *this* bread, can concentrate all his presence in a gift. . . . The consecrated bread incarnates the perfectly abandoned gift of a "body given for [us]" (Luke 22:19).[49]

God as Unoriginate Source of Love Revealed in Word and Enacted in Spirit

Love is interpersonal by definition. In applying Marion's shift from Being to Love to trinitarian thought, we move from thinking of Trinity in terms of Person to thinking of Trinity in terms of Love:

---

[44] Ibid., 21. Marion begins his reflections with the necessity of being loved, asking, "Does anybody love me?" (20), but then moves to the question, "Can I love first?" (71ff.), thus defining the essence of humanity as to be loved, but more important, to love.

[45] Ibid., 22–23.

[46] Ibid., 105–6.

[47] Marion, *Prolegomena to Charity*, 125.

[48] Ibid.

[49] Ibid., 133.

Unoriginate Source, eternally expressed in Word and enacted in Spirit.[50] In the reconfiguration of Trinity based on Marion's approach, our understanding of ourselves as persons made in the image and likeness of God and as coming from and having our being totally dependent upon God is exemplified in the person of Jesus Christ and the community formed by the Spirit.

In trinitarian theology the term *Person* has become an idol, a mirror and concept that limits and constrains the infinite. The word as a trinitarian concept is not bad in and of itself. Person is a legitimate and important part of the theological tradition, but we cannot escape our experience of what the word *person* means as it relates to human persons, and therefore, it has become a limit on the incomprehensibility of God. Our human concept and experience of the word is the reason the Trinity is so often pictured, both in art and in people's minds, as two men and a bird. As Marion argues for Being, Person captures what was experienced of the Divine "at a moment of a particular epoch"[51] in trinitarian theology, namely, the patristic era. The problem is that the word continues to be used, but the epoch has changed and, with it, the meaning of the word itself. Thus what was initially understood as naming the distinction of the Three becomes understood as three individual subjects with freedom and consciousness. I would agree with Marion that Person similarly "marks the extreme advance, then the reflected return, of a thought that renounces venturing beyond itself, into the aim of the invisible."[52] In other words, the language we use has become too literal in the human imagination. The word no longer moves us beyond concrete thinking into the infinite mystery of the incomprehensible. The word ends up restricting us to a finite image. Rather than finding ourselves created in the image of God, we

---

[50] The inspiration for this model of Trinity comes from the idea of triune consciousness using the concept of affect, cognition, and volition (see Heidi Russell, *The Heart of Rahner: The Theological Implications of Andrew Tallon's Theory of Triune Consciousness*, vol. 64 [Milwaukee: Marquette University Press, 2009], 234). A similar phenomenological approach to the concept of Trinity can be found in Anthony J. Kelly, *The Trinity of Love: A Theology of the Christian God* (Wilmington, DE: Michael Glazier, 1989). Also see Robert Doran, "The Starting Point of Systematic Theology," *Theological Studies* 67 (2006): 750–76, and "Addressing the Four-Point Hypothesis," *Theological Studies* 68 (2007): 674–82.

[51] Marion, *God without Being*, 30.

[52] Ibid.

create God in our image. We see our own reflection in the mirror of the word *Person*. Love, on the contrary, can function as icon, face, and gift. Person can be supplemented with the concept of Love as Source, Word, and Spirit. Perhaps Love even needs to be overemphasized to counteract the dangers of a literal interpretation of the word *Person*. The experience of love, as affective rather than cognitive, opens one to infinite potential depth and an experience of incomprehensibility which enables it to serve as icon.

Love is also a suitable analogy because it implies an infinite horizon. It is

> an advance that is definitive and without return, an advance that will never cancel itself out, and never catch up with itself. . . . For even if I reach the other, this does not give me possession, precisely because I only touch her and open an access to her by the impact that I provoke . . . ; the other does not stop me like a wall or an inert and delimited lump, but offers herself to me like a path that opens, always continuing in proportion to my entry forward.[53]

In other words, our human experience of love always implies movement. Like a horizon, we move toward the other, but the more we know of another person, the more we discover there is to know. We never reach the end of what we can know and love of another. Thus even in our encounters in which we do feel we touch the core of another person, we do not by that encounter possess that person, but rather it is like a new door or path opens inviting us even further into the mystery of who that person is. God as Love is infinite and ungraspable. That Love grounds human transcendence, opening us and luring us ever closer without ever becoming an object or a possession.

Love, and therefore relationality, precedes and defines personhood. Our entire being is dependent on its givenness. Marion notes: "Even that which is finds itself disqualified as if it were not, so long as it

[53] Marion, *The Erotic Phenomenon*, 83. Marion calls this phenomenon the erotic reduction. For the correlation with mystical theology, see 149–50. For an explanation of what Marion calls the "crossing of gazes" in love, see *Prolegomena to Charity*, 86–91; Karl Rahner, "Christian Dying," in *Theological Investigations: God and Revelation,* trans. Edward Quinn, vol. 18 (New York: Crossroad, 1983), 226–56.

does not have added to its status as a being the dignity of that which finds itself loved."[54] Like Marion's concept of being, our personhood is that of complete dependency, complete coming forth from another, and thus realized only in our realization and actualization of our interdependence. We come to be in love, and therefore we can only realize what it means to be made persons in the image and likeness of God in relationship and community, not because *God* is a community of three persons, but because God is self-gift and reveals Godself to be an outpouring of love and self in the cross. We come to understand what it means to be person, in the sense of a being that comes from and is totally dependent on love, in the incarnation of Jesus Christ.

God is Love, Unoriginate Source revealed in Word and enacted in Spirit. The Father is the Source, the "fountain" (to use a term from Bonaventure[55]) of Love that flows outward in self-expression and action. The Word is the eternal self-expression, revelation, and self-gift of Love. The Spirit is the eternal action, dynamism, and power of Love. This immanent Trinity, the technical term for who God is in Godself, is revealed in God's relationship to us, that is, in technical terms, the economic Trinity. However, the economic Trinity does not simply reveal God; it also reveals humanity because it reveals God in relationship to us. The immanent Trinity is revealed in the face of the economic Trinity. The invisible and infinite source of all Love is revealed in the face of Jesus the Christ and in the face of the other, those human persons in whom we encounter the indwelling Spirit, thus enabling us to realize and recognize the Spirit indwelling in our own person.

The Word of Love expressed in the incarnate Christ is *the* icon of God, who is Source of All Love. The icon reveals the infinite depth that cannot be grasped or comprehended. As Marion puts it, "The

---

[54] Marion, *God without Being*, xxvi.

[55] Bonaventure, "The Soul's Journey into God," in *Bonaventure: The Soul's Journey into God, the Tree of Life, the Life of Saint Francis*, ed. Ewert Cousins (New York: Paulist Press, 1978), 51–116. In the introduction Cousins notes: "Bonaventure begins his speculative trinitarian theology with the Father as the fountain-source of divine fecundity. For Bonaventure the Father is fountain-fulness, *fontalis plenitudo*, in whom the divinity is fecund, dynamic, self-expressive" (24–25). Cites *Commentarius in I, II, III, IV librum Sententiarum, I Sent.*, d. 27, p. 1, a. un., q.2 (I, 468–74); cf. *I Sent.*, d. 11, a. un., q. 2 (I, 214–16). See also Ilia Delio, "Theology, Metaphysics, and the Centrality of Christ," *Theological Studies* 68, no. 2 (2007): 228–54.

icon, which unbalances human sight in order to engulf it in infinite depth, marks such an advance of God that even in times of the worst distress indifference cannot ruin it. For, to give itself to be seen, the icon needs only itself. This is why it indeed can demand, patiently, that one receive its abandon."[56] Only Love is such that it gives itself in such a way that demands but is not dependent on its reception. Marion explains that "the inevitable impotence of man to correspond to the destiny that love gratuitously imposes upon him is not enough to disqualify its initiative or its accomplishment."[57] God as Love revealed in the incarnation and cross demands a response from us, but our lack of response or a feeble response does not and cannot diminish or annul the accomplishment of that love.

One understands *person* by understanding the incarnate Love found in Jesus Christ. We discover what it means to be person when we give ourselves in love to the other, when we take up our cross and are willing to sacrifice our individuality and our life for the sake of Love.[58] Thus to be person as Jesus Christ is person is not to be an independent individual caught up in our own interiority. Rather, to be person is to discover ourselves in relationship, in the giving of ourselves to another in Love. We are persons only in community and in the experience of intersubjectivity. We understand community in and through the recognition of mutuality and interrelationship formed by the indwelling Spirit creating us to be the body of Christ. There is a need to redefine the concept of person in light of Triune God, but we do so not from the aspect of Three Persons of the Trinity in fellowship and communion but rather from the understanding of God

---

[56] Marion, *God without Being*, 24.

[57] Ibid., 47–48.

[58] *Individuality* is used here in the sense of a lack of interconnectedness, not in the sense of one's uniqueness. A word of caution is necessary here in line with concerns of feminist theology, that the idea of a giving up selfhood for others, particularly in relationships of love, has been a concept that has been used to disempower women. However, understanding God as Love should enable us to have a healthier understanding of love in our own human relationships where it is not used as a power dynamic. As Karl Rahner notes in his axiom on human freedom, surrender to God/Love has a relationship of direct proportion to human freedom. Thus the more one gives oneself to this Love that is God and lets go of a clinging to individual existence, the more one becomes oneself, the truly unique individual in relationship one was created to be.

as Unoriginate Source of Love revealed in the person of Jesus Christ and enacted in the world by the Holy Spirit.

Love united to creation reveals what it means to be a human person in the humanity of Jesus as the face of Love incarnate. Love enacted in creation reveals what it means to be community in the action of Love moving in the Christian community awakening us to recognize the Spirit indwelling in the other. The Spirit forms the church into the body of Christ. One cannot be a member of that body without recognizing the indwelling Spirit in the other that is necessary for one's own union with Christ. Union is no longer a solitary venture. The Spirit demands alterity and interconnectedness. How do we become persons in Christ? Through the indwelling of the Holy Spirit, God as Love present and acting in us, forming us in communion into the body of Christ.

In the following chapters of this book, we look to reclaim images that support a more monotheistic understanding of Trinity as Love as found in scripture and the theological tradition. Primary among these is my suggestion of God as Source of Love, revealed as Word of Love, and enacted as Spirit of Love.

Chapter 3

The Trinity and Scripture

God of the Hebrew Scriptures

To understand the development of the Trinity in the Christian scriptures, one must first understand the development of monotheism in the Hebrew scriptures. While we believe that God has revealed Godself to us in and through the scriptures, those scriptures also show the development of our thought about God and our relationship to God throughout history in a process of theological reflection. Mark Smith points out that biblical language about God is "intensively metaphorical," noting that "we can barely think of an image for God in the Bible that is not a metaphor based on human experience of nature or society."[1]

The Hebrew scriptures (what we often call the Old Testament) do not give us a picture of unambiguous belief in the existence of only one God, or monotheism, as it has come to be called. Rather, the theological worldview in the Hebrew scriptures is polytheistic (belief in multiple gods) and/or henotheistic (primacy of one god among multiple gods) in the earliest passages, and possibly even in the later passages. Smith warns us not to be too facile in our distinctions, however, noting that discussions of polytheism and monotheism in the Ancient Near East "never asked what the 'oneness' or conceptual coherence of polytheism was for the ancient polytheists, or whether

[1] Mark S. Smith, *The Memoirs of God: History, Memory, and the Experience of the Divine in Ancient Israel* (Minneapolis: Fortress Press, 2004), 86.

and how monotheism was a reformulation of polytheism. It was simply assumed that monotheism differs radically from polytheism, and that monotheism was radically superior."[2] Smith argues that there is both a monism or a oneness to polytheism and "something quite poly about monotheism" as it emerges in ancient Israel.[3]

The ancient Israelites were a tribal people with a tribal God. Their God was the God of their tribe. Other tribes had other gods. The Israelites did not deny the existence of those other gods, but their primary relationship was to their God(s). Their relationship to their God(s) evolved as they evolved as a people.

John McKenzie explains that "settled people can worship a national god associated with a particular region, but nomads need a personal or clan god who goes with them."[4] As they develop into a nation, this concept of a clan God evolves into a national God. Jewish scholar Herbert Cohn explains:

> Out of the clans grew nations, and the household gods became national gods. In biblical times, each nation had its own gods, who were believed to protect the land and its inhabitants. Of course, each nation believed that its gods were stronger and mightier than those of their neighbors. . . . No nation put into doubt the existence of the gods of its neighbors, ancient Israel included. For the Israelite religion in those days, "the other gods" were realities protecting their respective countries. Like every nation, ancient Israel was also convinced that its God, the Eternal, was stronger and mightier than all the others.[5]

In the transition from nomadic tribes to a nation, their worship of their God, YHWH, becomes tied to the land as well. Recall the story in which Naaman, the commander of the Aram army, is cured of leprosy by the prophet Elisha. He asks for as much dirt as he can carry on his mules to take back with him to Aram, so that he can worship YHWH

---

[2] Ibid., 87.

[3] Ibid., 88.

[4] John L. McKenzie, "Aspects of Old Testament Thought," in *The New Jerome Biblical Commentary*, ed. Raymond Brown, Joseph Fitzmyer, and Roland Murphy (Englewood Cliffs, NJ: Prentice Hall, 1990), 1287.

[5] Herbert Cohn, "From Monolatry to Monotheism," *Jewish Bible Quarterly* 26, no. 2 (1998): 124.

in Aram, demonstrating this belief that one must be on the soil of a particular god in order to worship that god (2 Kgs 5).

Most scholars agree today that the Hebrew scriptures combined with archeological research tell a story of a people who were polytheistic in their worship practices, worshiping multiple gods and goddesses. Eventually, they develop a primary worship of YHWH, while not denying the existence of other gods and goddesses.[6] The early Israelite worship is most likely influenced by the worship of the surrounding Canaanite culture. Gary Anderson explains: "Among the deities of ancient Canaan, the most important was El, the chief god of the tribal clan, who directed the wars of his patrons and intervened on behalf of childless couples. He also presided over the 'council of gods,' which convened on his holy mountain. El was both the father of these gods and their leader."[7] In the Hebrew scriptures we find the repeated use of *El* to refer to God, as well as titles including *El*, such as *El Elyôn* (God Most High) or *El Shaddai* (God of the Mountains or God Almighty).[8] Passages such as Deuteronomy 32:8–9 parallel the Canaanite understanding of God:

> When the Most High [*Elyon*] apportioned the
> nations,
> when he divided humankind,
> he fixed the boundaries of the peoples
> according to the number of the gods [literally,
> sons of God];
> the LORD's [YHWH's] own portion was his people,
> Jacob his allotted share.

We see similar references in Psalm 82:1:

---

[6] Robert Gnuse, "The Emergence of Monotheism in Ancient Israel: A Survey of Recent Scholarship," *Religion* 29, no. 4 (1999): 315–36.

[7] Gary Anderson, "Introduction to Israelite Religion," in *The New Interpreter's Bible: A Commentary in Twelve Volumes*, ed. Leander Keck et al., vol. 1 (Nashville: Abingdon Press, 1994), 273.

[8] Note that some scholars argue that these names are not titles for the worship of *El*, but rather separate gods worshiped in their own right in a polytheistic manner. See Gnuse, "The Emergence of Monotheism in Ancient Israel," 315–36.

God [*elohoim*] has taken his place in the divine
council [of *El*];
in the midst of the gods [*elohim*] he holds
judgment,

and Psalm 89:6–8,

For who in the skies can be compared to the LORD
[YHWH]?
Who among the heavenly beings is like the
LORD [YHWH],
a God feared in the council of the holy ones,
great and awesome above all that are around him?

O LORD God of hosts,
who is as mighty as you, O LORD?
Your faithfulness surrounds you.

Smith explains that the Israelites most likely shared the familial structure of their pantheon of gods with the Ugaritic texts, with the Level 1 gods consisting of the divine parents, El and Asherah, and Level 2 the children, among whom is Yahweh.[9] Thus, he interprets the preceding passages to reflect earlier versions of these poems that would have referred to these two levels, El and YHWH. In these earlier versions YHWH is the tribal god of Israel, and El is the head of the divine council, but YHWH is eventually given the territories belonging to the gods of the other tribes.[10] Psalm 82 reads,

God [referring to El] has taken his place in the
divine council;
in the midst of the gods he holds judgement.

. . .

I [El] say, "You are gods,
children of the Most High [El] all of you;

[9] Smith, *The Memoirs of God*, 106–10. Smith notes that there does not seem to be evidence of Level 3 craftsmen gods, as there are in the Ugaritic texts, but does not rule them out for that reason. Level 4 gods are the household workers, such as the angels or divine messengers.

[10] Ibid., 107–9.

> nevertheless, you shall die like mortals,
> and fall like any prince."
>
> Rise up, O God [referring to YHWH], judge the earth; for all the nations belong to you! (Ps. 82:1, 6–8).

Smith explains:

> Psalm 82 preserves a tradition that casts the god of Israel [YHWH] not in the role of the presiding god of the pantheon, but implicitly as one of the sons. Each of these sons has a different nation as his family inheritance and therefore serves as its ruler. Yet verse 8 calls on Yahweh to take over the traditional inheritance of all the other gods, thereby making not only Israel but all the world into the inheritance of Israel's God. Psalm 82 is a polemic directed against the old worldview, which would suggest that the older worldview retains some force for the author of Psalm 82.[11]

In other words, we see in this psalm evidence of a transition from thinking of YHWH as one among many tribal gods to thinking of YHWH as the highest or even the only surviving tribal god, since verse 7 says these other gods will die like mortals. Likewise, as Deuteronomy 32 is written at a later time, the author probably does identify Elyon and YHWH, but Smith suggests that it echoes an earlier era in which they would not have been identified, but rather understood to be two different gods on two different levels of divinity—El as Father and head of the divine council/assembly, and YHWH as son and member of the divine council/assembly. He notes that by the time of the monarchy or even earlier, the two were identified as the one God of Israel, a Level 1 deity with a wife, Asherah.[12] Smith explains that the Level 2 deities are now the astral bodies of the sun, the moon,

---

[11] Ibid.

[12] Ibid., 110. Smith notes that there is debate about whether or not the references to Asherah in both scripture and archeology refer to Yahweh's consort, another symbol for Yahweh, or a reference to Yahweh's shrine, but adds that the majority of scholars view the references as referring to Yahweh's wife-consort.

the stars, and the heavenly host, skipping Level 3, followed by the Level 4 heavenly messengers such as the angels. Smith suggests that it is only with the dissolution of the family unit due to the ravages of exile that the idea of a divine household falls away to be replaced by the idea of a singular godhead who is "disconnected from the realm of death and lacking in sexual relations. Holier than the holy of holies, this god would model the ideal for priests and even the priestly people of Israel."[13] Thus, of the original levels of the divine household, only two remained: YHWH, who was the only divine power, and his heavenly messengers, the angels, who manifest that power on earth.[14] This "divine voice that issues the Torah . . . remains virtually unknown and unapproachable, except through observance and prayer."[15] This monotheism becomes read back and remembered back into the whole history of Israel's relationship with God that we find in scripture.

The earliest assertions that the Lord (YHWH) alone is God simply state the primacy of their God, the God of their fathers, the God of their tribe. One can speak here of monolatry, the exclusive worship of one God, more than monotheism as the existence of only one God.[16] In fact, some scholars today argue that there is no monotheism in the sense of a belief in the existence of only one God until Jewish theology encounters the concepts of Hellenistic philosophy as late as the second century BCE.[17]

---

[13] Ibid., 121, 123.

[14] Ibid., 141.

[15] Ibid.

[16] Note that this concept of an evolving monotheism in Judaism is not without debate. See Michael S. Heiser, "Monotheism, Polytheism, Monolatry, or Henotheism? Toward an Assessment of Divine Plurality in the Hebrew Bible," *Bulletin for Biblical Research* 18, no. 1 (2008): 1–30; Jens-André P. Herbener, "On the Term 'Monotheism,'" *Numen* 60, no. 5–6 (2013): 616–48; Matthew J. Lynch, "Mapping Monotheism: Modes of Monotheistic Rhetoric in the Hebrew Bible," *Vetus Testamentum* 64, no. 1 (2014): 47–68.

[17] For example, Heiser argues that the later passages in the Hebrew scriptures and in Second Temple literature that refer to the divine council of gods cannot be argued away as references to idols or humans, that in fact the idea of the existence of multiple gods persists into the Second Temple period of Judaism, and the scriptural declarations that there are no other gods than YHWH are assertions of YHWH's primacy among the gods and the requirement for exclusive worship, not claims that YHWH is the only God who exists. Heiser ultimately argues that neither monotheism, which he notes is a

The Israelites experience their unique relationship to their God, the God who becomes their only God, in and through their history. The primary example of this relationship to God is the experience of the Exodus from Egypt, when God liberates the people from slavery and forms them into Israel, a nation or confederation of tribes. Thus the primary image of God is God as Savior. God is understood as creator first and foremost in this act of creating a people, Israel. From this experience of God present and active in their own history, the Israelites come to understand God to be God of *all* history. They view God as creator of the world as well as the creator of the other gods. Eventually, belief in this God who created all the world and who reigns over all history became the belief that this God is the only God that exists, monotheism as we understand it today. Then we read the proclamation of God that "I am God; and there is no other" (Is 45:22). The other gods of neighboring nations are disparaged as idols made by human hands out of wood and metal, able to mold or rust, unable to hear prayers or speak (Is 45; Ps 115, Bar 6).

The Sacred Name of God—YHWH and *Iēsous*

The key revelation of God and relationship to God that is established in the events leading up to the Exodus (the stories of the patriarchs found in Genesis) and culminating in the Exodus event itself is the name of God, YHWH. This name of God is referred to as the "tetragrammaton," because the name consists of four letters of the Hebrew alphabet. This divine name is unpronounceable and untranslatable. God first identifies Godself to Moses in terms of historical context and relationship: "I am the God of your father, the God of Abraham, the God of Isaac, and the God of Jacob." (Ex 3:6). Note again the tribal pattern of naming God; God is a household or clan God. Then God goes on, at Moses's prompting, to reveal the divine name:

> God said to Moses, "I AM WHO I AM" (*'ehyeh asher 'ehyeh*). He said further, "Thus you shall say to the Israelites, 'I AM has sent me to you.'" God also said to Moses, "Thus you shall say

---

seventeenth-century term, nor henotheism or monolatry is an adequate term to describe what the scriptures portray as Israel's belief in YHWH. Heiser, "Monotheism, Polytheism, Monolatry, or Henotheism?" 1–30.

> to the Israelites, 'The Lord (*yhwh*), the God of your ancestors, the God of Abraham, the God of Isaac, and the God of Jacob, has sent me to you."
>
> This is my name forever,
> and this is my title for all generations. (Ex 3:14–15)

Later, in Exodus 6:2–3, we read, "God also spoke to Moses and said to him: I am the Lord. I appeared to Abraham, Isaac, and Jacob as God Almighty, but by my name, 'The Lord' I did not make myself known to them." The divine name becomes central to Israelite worship, and this concept of the divine name is later used in the New Testament writings and applied to Jesus.

In *An Introduction to the Trinity* Declan Marmion and Rik Van Nieuwenhove make the point that the Hebrew root of *to be* that is used in these passages giving the divine name YHWH does not refer to *being* in a metaphysical sense, but rather *to be* in the sense of "to be effective" or "to effect,"[18] or alternatively by other authors as "to cause to be."[19] The phrases allude to the active presence of YHWH in and with the people. R. Kendall Soulen notes that the phrases "I am who I am" and "I am" of verse 14 are often the focus of discussions about this passage, but in fact these titles are just commentary on the divine name, YHWH, which is given in verse 15.[20] The name given in verse 15 is not "I am" (*'ehyeh*), as is often thought. The name of God is so sacred that it is not even pronounced/cannot be pronounced, despite the popular tendency to say "Yahweh." The word *adonai*, which we translate "Lord," is generally said in its place. *Adonai* was a term used to address a king, and as we explore below, one of the most common images used for YHWH was that of king. In the Hebrew texts, the divine name was also demarcated in various textual ways (for example, written in Archaic Hebrew or with a special ink or replaced with a symbol) as a way of reverencing the name, but also as a reminder to those proclaiming the text not to say the name aloud, but rather to say the surrogate word in its place.[21] Our English translations generally

[18] Declan Marmion and Rik Van Nieuwenhove, *An Introduction to the Trinity* (Cambridge: Cambridge University Press, 2011), 36.

[19] See McKenzie, "Aspects of Old Testament Thought," 1286.

[20] R. Kendall Soulen, *The Divine Name(s) and the Holy Trinity,* vol. 1, *Distinguishing the Voices* (Louisville, KY: Westminster John Knox Press, 2011), 140.

[21] Ibid., 30.

continue this practice by using "LORD" in place of YHWH. This practice of setting apart the divine name by means of special appearance, Soulen argues, is very important in regard to the ways in which the New Testament writers also highlight certain words and titles.[22]

Soulen explains that "almost from the beginning of the Jesus movement, church connected scribes developed their own distinctive counterpart to Jewish scribal practice. They consistently marked off certain words from their surroundings by abbreviating them and drawing a line over the characters that remained. These words have become known as the *nomina sacra*, the holy or sacred names."[23] These *nomina sacra* included the Greek words for Lord (*Kyrios*), God (*Theos*), Jesus (*Iēsous*), and Christ (*Christos*).[24] Not only is the use of *nomina sacra* to refer to Jesus important, but even more significantly, Lord as a *nomen sacrum* is used in the Christian scriptures both to refer to the tetragrammaton and to refer to Christ.[25] In understanding the early Christian perspective on both the divinity of Christ and the understanding of that divinity within the framework of monotheism, one of the most important passages is 1 Corinthians 8:6: "Yet for us there is one God, the Father, from whom are all things and for whom we exist, and one Lord, Jesus Christ, through whom are all things and through whom we exist." In this passage Soulen notes that the words *God, Lord, Jesus*, and *Christ* are all *nomina sacra*.[26] This passage is traditionally interpreted as Paul's expression of the Jewish Shema from Deuteronomy 6:4, "Hear, O Israel: The LORD is our God, the LORD alone!" where the first clause is applied to God the Father, and the second clause is applied to the Lord (*Kyrios*), Jesus Christ.[27] Gerald O'Collins points out that the Greek word *kyrios* could mean many things from a polite form of address like "Sir" to the reference to the tetragrammaton.[28] Soulen highlights the fact that the use of the

---

[22] Ibid., 32ff.

[23] Ibid.

[24] Ibid.

[25] Ibid., 33–34. Soulen suggests that the reason *Kyrios* is written in place of the tetragrammaton in the Christian scriptures is due to the fact that the Christian tradition is originally an oral tradition, and the tetragrammaton is pronounced as *Kyrios*, which was later written down as it was said.

[26] Ibid., 35.

[27] Ibid. See also Gerald O'Collins, *The Tripersonal God: Understanding and Interpreting the Trinity* (New York: Paulist Press, 1999), 55–56.

[28] Ibid., 57.

nomen sacrum in writing Lord/*Kyrios* in reference to Christ implies the connection to the tetragrammaton. Soulen notes that the essentially binatarian nature of this Pauline passage in First Corinthians is expanded by the inclusion of the word Spirit (*pneuma*) among the *nomina sacra* in passages such as 2 Corinthians 13:13, "The grace of the Lord Jesus Christ, the love of God, and the communion of the Holy Spirit be with all of you," where in addition to *Lord, Jesus, Christ,* and *God,* the word *Spirit* is also highlighted as a *nomen sacrum.* Critics would point out that in addition to these words that seem to refer to God, Christ, and Spirit, other words such as *human being* and *cross* are highlighted in this way as well, but Soulen argues that those words are either words that are meant to highlight a theological point, such as the emphasis on Jesus's humanity against the gnostic teaching, or are used in combination with other words to create divine titles, such as *heaven* when used in conjunction with "our Father in heaven."[29]

God as Word, Wisdom, Spirit

The divine name of the tetragrammaton in the Hebrew scriptures, as one that is unpronounceable and untranslatable, points to God as incomprehensible mystery, to God's utter transcendence. At the same time the Hebrew scriptures also portray God as present to and interactive with God's creation, what is called God's immanence or nearness to creation. One way in which the Hebrew scriptures do so is to use images of God's Word, Wisdom, and Spirit to express this immanence. These words portray God's activity in creation and at times are even personified and anthropomorphized to express this nearness (imaged as humanlike figures, for example, Lady Wisdom in Proverbs 1:20). James Dunn explains, "God in himself is unknowable, but has made himself known in, through, and as his wisdom and rational power; which is to say that the Wisdom of God and Word of God in Jewish thought are simply God insofar as he reveals himself to humans and insofar as he can be known by humans."[30] While these

[29] Soulen, *The Divine Name(s),* 36–37. For a collection of critical reviews of this work along with Soulen's response, see *Pro Ecclesia* 23, no. 1 (2014): 22–80.

[30] James D. G. Dunn, "Was Christianity a Monotheistic Faith from the Beginning?" in *The Christ and the Spirit*, vol. 1, *Christology* (Grand Rapids, MI: Eerdmans, 1998), 331.

writings are not themselves expressing a triune God, this pattern of expressing God's nearness through these images of Word, Wisdom, and Spirit becomes central to the New Testament and early Christian ways of expressing the Trinity.[31] In other words, the followers of Christ have experiences of God in Christ, particularly in his death and resurrection, and in the reception of the Spirit. In seeking to express these experiences, they turn to the images and categories most familiar to them from the Hebrew scriptures.

In the Hebrew scriptures, one of the ways in which God expresses God's immanence is through God's Word (*dabar*). McKenzie explains the importance of the Word in the Ancient Near East's oral culture. He notes that the divine word is a creative force that cannot be altered, as it partakes of the power of the gods themselves. But even the human word was understood as holding power in terms of the ability to bless and curse, to promise and make contracts.[32] A word effects what it says. McKenzie reminds us of Jacob deceiving Isaac into giving him the blessing that rightly belonged to Esau.[33] Once it has been said, Isaac cannot undo it. All he can do is give Esau a different blessing.

In addition to the familiar story of creation in Genesis, in which God speaks the Word (God said, "Let there be . . . ") and what is spoken comes to be, the Word of God is also portrayed as an agent or instrument of creation in the Psalms and in Isaiah. Psalm 33:6, 9 states:

> By the word of the LORD the heavens were made,
> and all their host by the breath of his
> mouth. . . .
> For he spoke, and it came to be;
> he commanded, and it stood firm.[34]

---

[31] While Dunn argues in favor of a strict monotheism in the Hebrew scriptures, rejecting the notion of the personifications being actual divine agents or intermediaries in Judaism, he notes with irony that even those authors who similarly reject such a notion fall into the trap of using the language "of mythical figures, divine agents, heavenly redeemers, and intermediary beings" (ibid., 318). In respecting the integrity of the Hebrew scriptures, reading these personifications as beings or persons or anything other than the expression of God's own immanent presence to the people Israel should be avoided.

[32] McKenzie, "Aspects of Old Testament Thought," 1291.

[33] Ibid.

[34] See O'Collins, *The Tripersonal God*, 31; see also Ps 148:5; Wis 9:1; and Jdt 16:14.

The Word of God not only is an instrument and/or agent of creation but also is operative in conserving creation, holding all things together (Sir 43:26).[35] Likewise, the author of Isaiah 55 images God's Word as being effective: "so shall my word be that goes out from my mouth; it shall not return to me empty, but it shall accomplish that which I purpose, and succeed in the thing for which I sent it" (v. 11). Marmion and Van Nieuwenhove describe this Word in Isaiah as issuing from YHWH, accomplishing what YHWH intends, and returning to YHWH, a pattern we will see ascribed to Jesus in his incarnation, death, resurrection, and ascension in the Gospels.[36] They go on to explain:

> The Word expresses God's will for a specific situation; to experience its closeness one has "only to carry it out" (Deut. 30:14). The Word of God is not, however, a bald statement of divine will; it assumes an ongoing relationship, a communication between God and people. It is a personal and invading Word spoken in a specific encounter (e.g., the call of Jeremiah and Amos). God's Word can reflect inner-divine reflections or emotions (Gen. 2:18; 8:21), while the manifestations of God's word range from the spectacular to the unobtrusive, including visions and dreams.[37]

God's Word acts both directly, as in creation, and indirectly, as in the revelation to the prophets who speak in God's name, proclaiming, "Thus says the Lord." When God's Word is expressed through the prophets, the prophets take part in the power of God's Word, so that "the word is an entity endowed with power that effects the thing signified by the word."[38] Gerald O'Collins explains that God's Word is often used in conjunction with God's Spirit and/or God's Wisdom in "expressing God's creative, revelatory, and salvific activity."[39]

The image of God's Wisdom is even more developed than the image of God's Word, in that she is personified and speaks in the first person. Wisdom (*hokmah*) is referred to as begotten of God, firstborn,

---

[35] O'Collins, *The Tripersonal God*, 31.

[36] Marmion and Van Nieuwenhove, *An Introduction to the Trinity*, 30.

[37] Ibid., 31.

[38] McKenzie, "Aspects of Old Testament Thought," 1292.

[39] O'Collins, *The Tripersonal God*, 31.

present at and active in God's creating act (Prov 8:22–31; Wis 9:1–2). In the Book of Wisdom, Solomon prays for Wisdom and describes her as follows:

> For wisdom is more mobile than any motion;
> because of her pureness she pervades and penetrates
> all things.
> For she is a breath of the power of God,
> and a pure emanation of the glory of the Almighty;
> therefore nothing defiled gains entrance into her.
> For she is a reflection of eternal light,
> a spotless mirror of the working of God,
> and an image of his goodness.
> Although she is but one, she can do all things,
> and while remaining in herself, she renews all
> things;
> in every generation she passes into holy souls
> and makes them friends of God, and prophets.
> (Wis 7:24–27)

These images of Wisdom as the reflection of God's light, mirror of God's power, and image of God's goodness are used by the New Testament writers to speak of Jesus. Solomon goes on to pray:

> With you is wisdom, she who knows your works
> and was present when you made the world;
> she understands what is pleasing in your sight
> and what is right according to your commandments.
> Send her forth from the holy heavens,
> and from the throne of your glory send her,
> that she may labour at my side,
> and that I may learn what is pleasing to you.
> For she knows and understands all things,
> and she will guide me wisely in my actions
> and guard me with her glory. (Wis 9:9–11)

Wisdom is paired with God's Spirit (9:17) and God's Word (9:1). The images of feast and banquet (Prov 9:1–6) as well as hungering and thirsting (Sir 24:21) are also applied to Wisdom. These themes will be picked up in the gospel descriptions of Jesus's ministry of table fellowship.[40] As the presence or image or agent of God's immanence, Wisdom is understood to abide with the people Israel. She pitches her tent and dwells in Jacob/Israel. We hear this language echoing in the prologue to John's Gospel, in which the Word makes his dwelling—literally, "pitches his tent"—among us. Wisdom is associated with renewing and governing creation (Wis 7:27; 8:1) and ultimately with God's saving deeds in delivering the Israelites from Egypt in the Exodus.[41] As we will see, Paul most directly identifies not just Christ, but Christ crucified, a scandal to the Jews and foolishness to the Gentiles, with the Wisdom and Power of God in 1 Corinthians 1:24.

The transcendent God's activity in the world is made manifest not only through God's Word and Wisdom, but also through God's Spirit (*ruah*) in the Hebrew scriptures. Again warning against making these images into distinct "persons," John McKenzie notes that "in the OT the spirit is not a personal being. It is a principle of action, not a subject. It belongs properly to Yahweh alone."[42] The Hebrew word *ruah* or spirit also means breath, wind, and inspiration. Hence the Spirit is seen as the "giver of life," so the Psalmist proclaims to God,

> When you hide your face, they are dismayed;
> when you take away their breath, they die
> and return to their dust.
> When you send forth your spirit, they are created;
> and you renew the face of the ground. (Ps 104:29–30)

The Spirit of God inspires the judges and the prophets, working in and through them to establish God's saving plan in the world.[43] O'Collins notes the close relationship among Spirit, Word, and Wisdom for speaking about God's activity in the world.[44] God creates by Word and

---

40 Ibid., 25–26; Marmion and Van Nieuwenhove, *An Introduction to the Trinity*, 32.

41 O'Collins, *The Tripersonal God*, 29.

42 McKenzie, "Aspects of Old Testament Thought," 1290.

43 Marmion and Van Nieuwenhove, *An Introduction to the Trinity*, 33, 31.

44 O'Collins, *The Tripersonal God*, 32.

Spirit; God sends the Spirit of Wisdom both to individuals (Solomon) and the community of Israel as a whole. O'Collins summarizes:

> Naming God as *Father, Son* (Word or Wisdom), and *Spirit* found its roots in the OT. There Wisdom, Word, and Spirit functioned, frequently synonymously, to acknowledge the transcendent God's nearness to the world and to the chosen people—a nearness that did not, however, compromise the divine transcendence, or that otherness that sets God "beyond" all other beings. In their creative, revelatory, and redemptive involvement, Wisdom, Word, and Spirit took on divine roles, while staying clearly within God's control. At times almost identified with God (e.g., Wis 7:25–26), they remained distinct in function (Wis 9:4). These notions were available for the followers of Jesus, when they set out to express the "economic" missions in salvation history of the Son (as Wisdom and Word) and of the Spirit, as well as their inseparable role in the creation and conservation of the whole universe.[45]

Word, Wisdom, and Spirit in the Christian Scriptures

The use of the metaphors of Word, Wisdom, and Spirit in the Christian scriptures helped the early followers of Jesus describe the experience of God they were having in and through their encounters with Jesus the risen Christ and the reception of the Spirit while staying within the bounds of Jewish monotheism. James Dunn points out that the first great christological debate was "not so much over christology as such, as over *theo*-logy, about the understanding of *God*, about *monotheism*. And even more important to realize that the belief which triumphed was the belief in God as one and in Jesus as the expression of the one God."[46] Gerald O'Collins points out that the ways in which the Hebrew scriptures used the images or even personifications of God's Word, Wisdom, and Spirit to express God's nearness to the world are used by the writers of the Christian scriptures to express

---

[45] Ibid.

[46] James D. G. Dunn, *The Partings of the Ways: Between Christianity and Judaism and Their Significance for the Character of Christianity* (Philadelphia: Trinity Press International, 1991), 241, 321.

the role of the Son/Word and Spirit in God's plan of salvation, as well as in the act of creation and sustaining/fulfilling that creation.[47]

Jesus is most explicitly identified with God's Word in the Prologue to John's Gospel: "In the beginning was the Word, and the Word was with God, and the Word was God" (1:1). In the Prologue, the Word is the agent of creation through whom all things came to be and have life (1:2–3). Like Wisdom in the Hebrew scriptures, that Word "dwells" with us (1:14). What distinguishes and eventually separates Christianity from Judaism is the assertion that in Jesus, this Word "became flesh" (1:14).[48]

The Pauline literature also draws heavily on the Wisdom and Spirit imagery. The crucified Christ is the wisdom and the power of God (1 Cor 1:18–24). The hymn in Colossians (1:15–20) describes Christ as the image of God, the firstborn of creation, and the agent through whom all was created (1:15–16).[49] Christ also sustains creation (1:17). O'Collins explains that the understanding of Christ as the agent of creation emerges from the early followers' experience of new life in Christ and the belief in a final new creation in and through the resurrection.[50]

When we read the Spirit imagery of the Christian scriptures, the references are often to the Spirit of Christ. Marmion and Van Nieuwenhove note:

> At times Paul does not clearly distinguish the Spirit from Christ. In Rom. 8:9–11, for example, he uses the terms 'Spirit of God', 'the Spirit of Christ', 'Christ', and 'the Spirit of him who raised Jesus from the dead' interchangeably when describing how God dwells in the Christian. Sometimes he speaks of a sending of the 'Spirit of the Son' (Gal. 4:6), or of the 'Spirit of Jesus Christ' (Phil. 1:39), while elsewhere he will even say, 'The Lord is the Spirit' (2 Cor. 3:17). Paul is likely asserting a functional identity between Christ and the Spirit in that the risen Christ is present wherever the Spirit acts.[51]

---

[47] O'Collins, *The Tripersonal God*, 32–33.
[48] Marmion and Van Nieuwenhove, *An Introduction to the Trinity*, 37.
[49] See also 2 Cor 4:4 and 1 Cor 8:6.
[50] O'Collins, *The Tripersonal God*, 30, 56.
[51] Marmion and Van Nieuwenhove, *An Introduction to the Trinity*, 46–47.

Rarely do we find references to the Spirit in the sense of a distinct *hypostases* or person. Veli-Matti Kärkkäinen refers to a New Testament binatarianism along with a Trinitarianism, meaning that some passages in the New Testament only seem to refer to the relationship of Father and Son, while others explicitly name the Holy Spirit as well.[52] He suggests, however, that the trinitarian consciousness is present even when not explicitly stated.[53] Kärkkäinen notes that in the Gospels, Jesus is conceived by the Spirit, anointed by the Spirit, and ministers by the power of the Spirit; in the Pauline material, he is raised from the dead by the Spirit.[54] That same Spirit is then said to indwell in believers, allowing them to also cry "Abba" and thus including them in the relationship between Father and Son, ultimately raising them from the dead as well.[55]

Marmion and Van Nieuvenhove show that the development of the role of the Spirit in the Christian scriptures is ultimately about the experience of the believer and the formation of the community. They summarize:

> If the redemption wrought by Christ provides the content or the "what" of the Gospel, then the Spirit is the "how." In the Spirit the *Christus incarnatus* becomes the *Christus praesens*. The Spirit actualises or makes real in the believer the objective redemption won by Christ. In short, the Spirit enables people to experience God. For Paul, the Spirit is not an object over and against us but breathes in us and through us. The Spirit is the enabler of faith or, changing metaphors, the light which enables the believer to see Christ.[56]

The doctrine of the Trinity is not something that is explicitly developed in scripture, but it is grounded in scripture and the naming of the experience of the earliest community of disciples.

---

[52] Veli-Matti Kärkkäinen, *The Trinity: Global Perspectives* (Louisville, KY: Westminster John Knox Press, 2007), 9, 14–15.

[53] Ibid.

[54] Ibid. See also O'Collins, *The Tripersonal God*, 35–42.

[55] Kärkkäinen, *The Trinity*, 409. See also Marmion and Van Nieuwenhove, *An Introduction to the Trinity*, 48.

[56] Marmion and Van Nieuwenhove, *An Introduction to the Trinity*, 46–47.

Father and Son

The final terminology that we want to explore in this brief overview of the scriptures is the use of the Father and Son language to refer to God and Jesus Christ. In doing so, it is important to understand the Jewish context of these terms as they were used in the Hebrew scriptures. While Father is not a common title used for God in the Hebrew scripture (King is the most common title after the tetragrammaton), Gerald O'Collins points out that it is used over twenty times.[57] God is referred to primarily as the Father of Israel (Dt 32:6), having formed Israel as a people in the Exodus and again in the care and concern shown for them in the exile (Jer 31:9). O'Collins points out that in this prophetic literature God becomes "our Father" who offers redemption and salvation (Is 63:16; 64:6–8).[58] God is also the Father of David or the Davidic king (2 Sm 12–15; Ps 89).[59] This image of God as Father is also used in the Wisdom literature of Tobit and Sirach.[60] Finally, God is the Father of the most vulnerable, the orphan (Ps. 68).[61]

As a corollary to the use of the title Father in the Hebrew scriptures, the title Son of God is used first and foremost to refer to Israel.[62] Israel is the firstborn Son of God, as we learn in the story of the Exodus: "Then you shall say to Pharaoh, 'Thus says the LORD: Israel is my firstborn son. I said to you, "Let my son go that he may worship me." But you refused to let him go; now I will kill your firstborn son'" (Ex 4:22–23). As the story of Israel, God's Son, unfolds, Israel proves to be disobedient to his Father. In the Christian scriptures, in contrast with Israel as the disobedient Son of God, Jesus is imaged as the obedient Son of God (see, for example, the account of the temptation of Jesus in the desert in Matthew 4).

The Davidic king was also known as the Son of God, as was a righteous man.[63] O'Collins connects the title Son of God to suffering:

---

57 O'Collins, *The Tripersonal God*, 13–14.

58 Ibid., 18.

59 Ibid., 16–17.

60 Ibid., 20.

61 Ibid., 16.

62 John Schmitt, "Israel as the Son of God in Torah," *Biblical Theology Bulletin* 34 (2004): 69–79.

63 O'Collins, *The Tripersonal God,* 21–22.

"In the OT story, the collective 'son of God,' the people repeatedly suffer, and so too do the righteous individuals who call God 'Father' (Wisdom 2:10–20)."[64] In Wisdom we read:

> Let us [the wicked] oppress the righteous poor
> man; . . .
> "Let us lie in wait for the righteous man,
> because he is inconvenient to us and opposes our
> actions. . . .
> He professes to have knowledge of God and calls
> himself a child of the Lord. . . .
> He calls the last end of the righteous happy,
> and boasts that God is his father.
> Let us see if his words are true,
> and let us test what will happen at the end of his
> life;
> for if the righteous man is God's child, he will
> help him,
> and will deliver him from the hand of his adversar-
> ies. . . .
>
> Let us condemn him to a shameful death,
> for, according to what he says, he will be protected."
> (Wis 2:10a, 12a, 13, 16b–18, 20)

This theme of the righteous Son of God suffering is clearly central to Christians applying the title and image to Jesus.

In the Christian scriptures Jesus addresses God as Abba. Kärkkäinen points out that this title is mistakenly explained as Daddy; in fact, Abba refers to a very intimate, but adult, relationship with God.[65] Perhaps Dad is a better expression of this relationship than either Daddy or Father. As the community of believers, we are drawn into this relationship between Abba and Son, becoming ourselves sons and daughters of God, also able to cry "Abba" by the power of the Spirit (Rom 8:14–17; Gal 4:5–7).

---

[64] Ibid., 59.

[65] Kärkkäinen, *The Trinity*, 13.

The Proclaimer Is Proclaimed

Ultimately, we see the clearest biblical expressions of the Trinity in the use of trinitarian formulas of commission (Mt 28:19) and blessing (2 Cor 13:13). These formulas were most likely used in the earliest liturgical traditions of the Christian community. As the theological axiom says, *Lex orandi, lex credendi*—as we pray, so we believe. The followers of Christ had an experience of God, YHWH, in Christ through his life and ministry, death, and resurrection. They had an experience of God, YHWH, in receiving the Spirit of Christ that joined them to Christ's mission, gave them a share of Christ's power and authority. Ultimately, the Spirit forms them into a community that is the body of Christ, the ongoing presence of God, YHWH, active and incarnate in the world. O'Collins summarizes:

> Paul continues to be monotheistic and does not abandon the Jewish faith in one God professed by the Shema (Dt 6:4). . . . At the same time, Paul's monotheism is Christological and pneumatological, and this is a new development. . . . Although we certainly do not find here (or even later in the NT) anything like the eventual, full-blown doctrine of God as three in one and one in three (Father, Son, and Holy Spirit), nevertheless, the Pauline teaching about the Trinity (based above all on the resurrection of the crucified Jesus and the coming of the Holy Spirit) and subsequent NT witness provide a foundation and a starting point for that doctrinal development.[66]

In Paul we find the great paradigm shift from Jesus preaching the gospel message, "The reign of God is at hand!" to Paul preaching the risen Christ. The gospel or good news for Paul is Christ crucified: "But we proclaim Christ crucified, a stumbling block to Jews and foolishness to Gentiles, but to those who are called, Jews and Greeks alike, Christ the power of God and the wisdom of God" (1 Cor 1:23–24). In the famous words of Rudolf Bultmann, "The proclaimer becomes the proclaimed."[67] Paul's great theological insight is his conviction that the community is the body of Christ, illustrated in

---

[66] O'Collins, *The Tripersonal God*, 69.

[67] Rudolf Bultmann, *Theology of the New Testament*, trans. Kendrick Grobel, vol. 1 (New York: Scribner, 1951), 33.

the narrative version of Paul's revelation of Christ found in Acts of the Apostles. We read the story of Paul, then known as Saul, on his way to Damascus. Suddenly, "he fell to the ground and heard a voice saying to him, 'Saul, Saul, why do you persecute me?' He asked, 'Who are you, Lord?' The reply came, 'I am Jesus, whom you are persecuting" (Acts 9:4–5). In his own words, Paul tells us nothing other than that he received the gospel through a revelation of Jesus Christ and that God called him and revealed to him God's Son (Gal 1:11–17).

The identification of the Christian community with the body of Christ is found throughout Paul's writings and most explicitly in 1 Corinthians 12. We become part of this one body by sharing in the one loaf (1 Cor 10) of the Eucharist. For Paul, catholicity or wholeness as love was what it meant to be the one body of Christ. As many parts of the one body of Christ, we have many gifts that differ (Rom 12:4–8). These gifts are given by the Spirit and are to be used for the building up of the whole community, not for the building up of the individual (1 Cor 12:4–11; Eph 4:11–16). In 1 Corinthians 14, Paul deals specifically with this issue in terms of the gift of speaking in tongues, noting that if there is no one to interpret the tongues, the gift does no good in the community. While speaking in tongues is not forbidden, gifts are meant to be judged and prioritized based on the extent to which they benefit the whole community. Likewise, the law becomes subjugated to the goodness of the community. One of Paul's main theological paradigm shifts is that one is not saved by following the law but through Christ alone. Thus, for Paul, the law becomes subject to the body of Christ, the community gathered. The law now is the primacy of love as revealed in the person of Jesus Christ. Following the purity laws of the Jewish tradition is not problematic in itself, but if it prevents one from sitting down to eat with one's Gentile-Christian brothers and sisters, then one must let go of the law in order to protect the integrity of the body of Christ, so that the whole community can share in the eucharistic meal (Rom 14). Eating meat sacrificed to idols is not an issue, so long as one does not believe in or sacrifice to the idols. However, if eating the sacrificed meat scandalizes one's Jewish-Christian brothers and sisters in the faith, one should refrain from doing so (1 Cor 10:31–33). When the rich feast and get drunk while being blind to the needs of the poor among them, they fail to recognize the body of Christ, and in doing so court God's wrath (1 Cor 11:17–29). The community of Corinth is living a fragmented existence instead of realizing the wholeness of love that is what it means to be the body of Christ.

One's actions are judged not by the law but by their effect on the community, their effect on the unity of the Spirit-formed body of Christ. One no longer needs to be a slave to the law because one now lives a life in the Spirit. The requirements of that life, which is a life lived in love and the wholeness of community, exceed the minimum requirements of the law. One is not a good person because one is following the law; rather, one is a good person because by the power of the Holy Spirit one is now united to Christ and exemplifies Christ's love in the world. For Paul, the Holy Spirit is the love of God poured into our hearts (Rom 5:5).

As trinitarian theology developed in the early centuries of Christianity, it had to stay grounded in this New Testament monotheism. Dunn notes:

> The main debates of the second century started with the recognition of the deity of Christ, as attempts to spell out the implications of Logos christology, with docetism or modalism as the main alternatives—attempts in other words to spell out the implications of a christology operating *within* monotheism, of a monotheistic christology. It was *the givenness of Christian monotheism*, already disputed but firmly maintained, which dictated the framework of these debates and the alternatives open to those who took a Wisdom-Logos christology for granted.[68]

The prior assumption of monotheism enabled subsequent questions about the relationship between the Father and the Son, as well as questions about the relationship of the humanity to the divinity in the Son, questions to which we return in Chapter 4.

---

[68] Dunn, *The Partings of the Ways*, 241.

Chapter 4

Patristic Images of the Trinity

Beginning in the second century, we move from an experience of Jesus the risen Christ celebrated and proclaimed in the liturgy to an attempt to explain the faith to others using new categories borrowed from Hellenistic philosophy. The bridge between the experience of the followers of Jesus and the philosophical systematization of theology is the liturgy—*lex orandi, lex credendi* (as we pray, so we believe).[1] Declan Marmion and Rik Van Nieuwenhove point out that as early as the writing of the story of Stephen in the Acts of the Apostles, early Christians had a tradition of calling on Jesus in prayer.[2] This tradition of prayer to Jesus and in the name of Jesus culminates with the Council of Nicaea in 325 CE articulating the doctrine of the consubstantial full divinity of the Son. Marmion and Van Nieuwenhove note that this doctrine marks "a shift in emphasis from the human Christ as mediator and High Priest in his humanity (Heb. 4:14–16) to the Son as the second Person of the Trinity and therefore a recipient of worship."[3] There is a shift from praying to God the Father *through* the Son to prayers like the *Gloria* that pray glory to the Father *and* the Son *and* the Spirit.[4] This connection between prayer and belief also influenced the doctrine of the Holy Spirit. In making the case for the primacy of the Holy Spirit in a trinitarian experience of prayer, Sarah

[1] For an in-depth discussion of this point, see Sarah Coakley, *God, Sexuality, and the Self: An Essay "On the Trinity"* (Cambridge: Cambridge University Press, 2013), 106ff.

[2] Declan Marmion and Rik Van Nieuwenhove, *An Introduction to the Trinity* (New York: Cambridge University Press, 2011), 54–55.

[3] Ibid., 57.

[4] Ibid., 57n13.

Coakley points out that "there is something, admittedly obscure, about the sustained activity of prayer that makes one want to claim that it is personally and divinely activated from within, and yet that that activation (the 'Spirit') is not quite *reducible* to that from which it flows (the 'Father')."[5] Key to this principle was the profession of faith in the Father, Son, and Holy Spirit professed in baptism. Already by the late first and early second century there were rules of faith *(regula fidei)* referenced in the writings of Irenaeus and Tertullian, among others who profess belief in a God who is Father, Son, and Spirit.[6] Guided by scripture and the tradition as they were found in these rules, the early theologians of the church freely borrowed from philosophy to explain their belief systems while at the same time rejecting aspects of those philosophies that ran counter to what they believed.

The questions and controversies of the second century begin with an assumption of the divinity of Christ and the assumption of monotheism. The questions asked now are how we understand the relationship between the Father and the Son (as well as the Spirit, though less attention is given to the Spirit in the earliest developments). This question dominates the conversation up through the Council of Nicaea. After the Council of Nicaea much of the debate centers on questions of Christology, which is to say, how one person can be both human and divine. This period culminates with the Council of Chalcedon in 451 CE, which proclaims the two natures of Christ in one person without change, without confusion, without division, and without separation.[7] This chapter touches on some significant images of the Trinity given to us in this early period, primarily in regard to

[5] Coakley, *God, Sexuality, and the Self*, 112.

[6] For a more in-depth discussion of the debates around the nature of these rules of faith, see Paul M. Blowers, "The Regula Fidei and the Narrative Character of Early Christian Faith," *Pro Ecclesia* 6, no. 2 (1997): 199–228.

[7] The other important councils are the Council of Constantinople in 381, which affirms that Christ has a human soul and affirms the divinity of the Holy Spirit; the Council of Ephesus in 431, which affirms that there is only one hypostasis (person or individual) in Christ; the Second Council of Constantinople in 553, which affirms that the one person in Christ is the person of the divine Logos; and the Third Council of Constantinople in 681, which affirms that with the two natures, Christ has two wills and two modes of action, thus affirming the full humanity of Christ. These six councils, together with the Second Council of Nicaea in 787, which deals with the iconoclast controversy, make up the seven ecumenical councils of the early church, and

the earlier issues of the relation of the Father and Son (and Spirit) and culminates in the Eastern understanding of the Trinity found in the Cappadocians and Maximus the Confessor.

The Influence of Greek Philosophy on the Doctrine of the Trinity

In order to understand the developments in trinitarian theology, one must understand some of the philosophies that were prevalent at the time. These philosophies were used by the early Christian theologians to explain and define Christian concepts, but they were also the foil against which Christian concepts were demarcated and defended. Primary among these philosophies are Platonism and Stoicism. Platonism itself developed over time, so that the influence of middle Platonism is different from the influence of the writings of Plotinus, often referred to as Neo-Platonism. They all involve a dualism that at best sees the material world as an obstacle to be overcome and at worst sees the material world as evil. Christianity today still struggles with vestiges of this suspicion of the material world as a result, even while pronouncing its goodness and the unity of body/spirit in the human person.

The Platonic worldview holds the idea of the One *(to Hen)* or the Good as absolutely transcendent and immutable, eternal and perfect, and the source of all that exists. The One eternally begets a perfect copy of itself, the *Nous* or the *Logos*, the mind/intellect or the reason of the One. The Christian theologian Origen borrows the language of "eternally begotten" from middle Platonism, words we still proclaim in the Creed to this day. The *Nous/Logos* is the Demiurge, the agent through which the One creates the world. Platonism also suggests a third order after the One and the *Nous/Logos*, and that is the Psyche or world-soul. The Psyche is a copy of the *Nous/Logos* and is the soul of the world and the intermediary between the world of spirit and the world of matter. For Plato, matter is eternal. Matter exists but in an unordered state. The *Nous/Logos*/Demiurge out of goodness creates the cosmos by ordering the previously unordered matter according to the paradigm or ideal pattern of the world.

---

their teachings are accepted by the Roman and Eastern Catholic Churches, the Orthodox Churches, and most mainline Protestant Churches.

The early Christian theologians take this schema of the One, the Logos, and the Psyche and use it to explain the Father, the Son/Word, and the Spirit. In this correlation the Father is the Source of all, absolutely transcendent and immutable. The Word or Logos is the agent of creation, eternally begotten of the Father. The Spirit is then associated with the Psyche, the intermediary between the material world and the spiritual world.

Stoicism also influenced the development of Christianity, particularly in terms of understanding the Word or Logos. The idea of the Logos in Stoicism is the rational order of the world. All things that exist participate in the Logos. Our human experience of reason or rationality is due to our participation in the Logos. Each of us possesses "seeds" of the Logos, or *logo spermikos*. This concept was borrowed by Christian theologians to explain both our participation in the Word of God as well as the way in which the seeds of the Logos were present in the world even prior to the incarnation. In this way they saw the pre-Christian philosophers as possessing these "seeds" even without knowledge of Christ and thus able to communicate some understanding of the Trinity without or prior to the revelation of the Trinity in Christ and the Spirit.

Platonism and Stoicism give early Christian theologians a basic structure from which they drew the earliest images of the Trinity. For the early apologists this Platonic hierarchy injects a subordinationism in the doctrine of the Trinity that is problematic—the Son is less than the Father, and the Spirit is less than the Son. At the same time, these philosophies provide a sliding scale of divinity that enables a belief in the divinity and oneness of the Three. God the Father is *ho Theos or proto Theos*, meaning "the God" or "the first God." The Son is the Demiurge, *deuteron theos*, or God in a derivative sense. And the Spirit is *tritero theos*, or a third level of divinity. All three are God, however, in a way that creation is not. There was a clear separation between God and that which is created.

Images of the Trinity in Patristic Theology

In the early centuries of Christian theology, trinitarian theology was being worked out in dialogue, albeit not always friendly dialogue. As Christians tried to articulate what is meant by Father, Son, and Spirit, and the relationship among them, disagreements arise and eventually church teaching is defined over and against ideas that were rejected as heretical. It is important to note that early "orthodox" theologians also held ideas, such as subordinationism, that would later come to be understood as heresy or incorrect teaching, but these theologians were not considered heretical in their time. The theology of the Trinity was worked out over time and through the exchange of ideas. In that process theologians used the culture and the philosophy of their time to try to articulate trinitarian concepts in the same way that theologians today use philosophy, social sciences, and natural sciences as dialogue partners to make theological concepts vibrant and relevant in the context of our worldview. While our journey through the patristic era cannot be exhaustive, we explore some of the key images and concepts that continue to ground and inspire trinitarian theology today.

Justin Martyr (c. 100–165 CE)

Justin Martyr is one of the early apologists, meaning that he took Christian concepts and attempted to make them intelligible to the Greek-speaking, non-Jewish world by using concepts from Hellenistic philosophy to articulate Christian ideas. Justin, influenced by Stoicism and Middle Platonism, maintained that the Father alone is unbegotten and unoriginated (another way of saying Source of All, in that the Father has no source) and the Son or Logos is "begotten before the created universe and the agent of all creation."[8] He reserved the Platonic and biblical *ho Theos* for the Father and uses the titles Son, Word, and Christ for that which is begotten.[9] The Holy Spirit is not always clearly delineated from the Son in his writings, and in fact he uses the titles Son, Word, and Lord for the Spirit at times, while also using images of Glory *(Shekinah)*, Wisdom, Angel of the Lord (from the Hebrew scriptures, a title Justin also uses for Jesus at times), or God for the Spirit.[10] There is a great fluidity in the way Justin uses these titles, interchanging them between Jesus and the Spirit. Justin's main concern is upholding monotheism and explaining the

[8] Gerald O'Collins, *The Tripersonal God: Understanding and Interpreting the Trinity* (New York: Paulist Press, 1999), 87.

[9] Ibid., 88.

[10] Ibid.

relationship between the Father and Son. To do so, he uses the image of the sun and its ray or of one fire kindling another fire, sharing the same essence or *ousia*.[11] When we say the Nicene Creed today, we use Justin's words "light from light." Justin describes the Father and Son as "distinct in number but not in mind."[12]

Gerald O'Collins points out that Justin adopted the Platonic and Stoic concept of *logos spermatikos*, or seeds of the Logos, recognizing "seeds" in all people operating as the principle of rationality or intelligibility as coming from God. He quotes Justin's *Second Apology*:

> Plato's teaching are not contrary to Christ's but they are not in all respects identical with them: as is the case with the doctrines of others, the Stoics, the poets, and the prose authors. For each through his share in the divine generative Logos, spoke well, seeing what was suited to his capacity. . . . Whatever has been spoken aright by anyone belongs to us Christians; for we worship and love, next to God, the Logos who is from the unbegotten and ineffable God. . . . All those writers were able, through the seed of the Logos implanted in them, to see reality darkly. For it is one thing to have the seed of a thing and to imitate it up to one's capacity; far different is the thing itself, shared and imitated in virtue of its own grace.[13]

As Christians today we continue to recognize the seeds of the Logos working in other religious and philosophical traditions, as well as in the social and natural sciences. Wherever knowledge, goodness, and love flourish, we see the seeds of the Logos at work in humanity, regardless of whether Christian or not, because all humanity was created in, through, and unto Christ and therefore participates in the eternal Logos. In this concept of the seeds of the Logos we see the interconnected nature of reality as an unfolding whole. O'Collins also notes that Origen later follows Justin in using the image of light; he maintains that God's rays are not limited to Jesus, but rather, one finds the Logos wherever light is found.[14] If we understand the wholeness

[11] Ibid., 89.
[12] Ibid., 90; cites Justin Martyr, *Dialogue* 56.
[13] Ibid., 92; cites Justin Martyr, *Second Apology*, 13.
[14] Ibid., 93.

of God as Love to be enfolded into all aspects of reality, we can see the ways in which the Spirit unfolds that whole. As Origen says, wherever light is found, one finds the Logos. We might say that wherever Love is found, the Spirit is unfolding the enfolded Logos given by the Source of All Love.

Irenaeus of Lyons (115–202 CE)

Irenaeus of Lyons goes further to describe the distinctions as being within God for all eternity and manifest in the economy. O'Collins explains that Ireneaus views "the Logos as eternally coexisting with the Father 'before' truly becoming flesh."[15] Irenaeus argues that while God is clearly revealed to be the source of all, how God produces the Son cannot be known.[16] He refers to the Son and the Spirit as the two hands of God the Father reaching down into the world: "For he has always at his side his Word and Wisdom, the Son and the Spirit. Through them and in them he created all things of his own free will."[17] God's Word and God's Wisdom are manifested as Son and Spirit in creation and redemption.[18] Irenaeus argues against the Gnostics, those who deny the humanity of Jesus, maintaining that the Word of God is made incarnate, suffers, and dies, and therefore Jesus of Nazareth and the Word of God are "one and the same."[19] Jesus is true man and true God.

Irenaeus understands the Word of God to be the revealer of God in the world. That Word reveals God's presence to all of creation. Thomas Torrance observes that Irenaeus finds "the central issue of the Gospel" to be "the incarnation of the very Word, Mind and Truth of God himself in Jesus Christ. 'Since it is impossible, without God, to come to knowledge of God, he teaches men through his Word to know

---

[15] Ibid., 96.

[16] Irenaeus, *Adversus Haereses (Against Heresies)*, hereafter AH, 2.28.6, cited in ibid., 98.

[17] AH 4.20.1., cited in ibid., 99 (as well as in most other texts referenced in this section).

[18] J. N. D. Kelly, *Early Christian Doctrines*, rev. ed. (New York: Harper, 1978), 104–5.

[19] O'Collins, *The Tripersonal God: Understanding and Interpreting the Trinity*, 101; cites AH, 3.8.2; 3.9.3; 3.17.4.

God.'"[20] Thus, not only are the great philosophers understood to participate in the Word through the use of reason, the Hebrew scriptures are also read through the lens of the Word revealing God's presence. The Old Testament theophanies are read as revelations by the Word, so that it is the Word who is revealed to Moses in the burning bush and who saves the Israelites.[21] We hear the echoes of this interpretation yet today when we proclaim the "O Antiphons"[22] each Advent, singing songs such as "O Come, O Come Immanuel"—"O come, O come, great Lord of might / who to your tribes on Sinai's height / in ancient times did give the law / in cloud and majesty and awe."[23]

The Spirit, as the Wisdom of God, then enables us to perceive and receive this revelation of the Word. The Spirit "prepares us" for the Son.[24] O'Collins also notes that for Irenaeus, the Spirit "is intimately linked with the church: 'Where the Church is, there is the Spirit of God; and where the Spirit of God is, there is the Church and every kind of grace.'"[25] Thus the Spirit makes us church.

Khaled Anatolios argues that, for Irenaeus, the Son and the Spirit are mediators of divine presence, not external to God, but rather "are themselves constitutive of this presence, power, and efficacy."[26] His point is that the Son and the Spirit are not separate individuals from God the Father, but rather are the way in which God manifests Godself to the world in God's creative and salvific activity. As Anatolios states, for Irenaeus, God does not need external instruments to relate to the world, because God has his hands, the Son and the Spirit,

---

[20] Thomas F. Torrance, *The Christian Doctrine of God: One Being Three Persons* (Edinburgh: T & T Clark, 1996), 77; cites AH 4.8.1.

[21] O'Collins, *The Tripersonal God,* 100.

[22] Ibid.

[23] The "O Antiphons" are used with the Magnificat during Evening Prayer the week leading up to Christmas. On December 18, the antiphon is "O Sacred Lord (*Adonai*) of Israel, who showed yourself to Moses in the burning bush, who gave him the law on Sinai mountain, come, stretch out your mighty hand to set us free." *Christian Prayer: The Liturgy of the Hours* (New York: Catholic Book Publishing, 1976), 121. Note also that the antiphon for December 17 is "O Wisdom, O Holy Word of God."

[24] O'Collins, *The Tripersonal God,* 121.

[25] Ibid.; citing AH 3.24.1.

[26] Khaled Anatolios, "The Immediately Triune God: A Patristic Response to Schleiermacher," *Pro Ecclesia* 10, no. 2 (2001): 169.

through which God relates to the world.[27] For Irenaeus, this argument is not so much about us and our creation as it is about God.[28] Creation must be related to God, because there is no "outside" of God's presence. If there were, then God would be limited. Anatolios states, "To posit a realm from which God is absent is to simultaneously limit the presence of such a God."[29] Likewise, God does not need external mediators or instruments to relate to creation, because God has no *need* of anything outside of God's self. If God did, God would be limited. The principles of creative and salvific activity and the means of God's mediation to the world are the Son and the Spirit, and they are a part of God's very self.

Irenaeus's vision of the relationship between God and the world is one in which God is the wholeness. There is no outside of God. There is no limit or boundary to God. God is the whole. That whole then unfolds in Trinity, the two hands of God interconnecting all of creation. Irenaeus maintains that the entire created world will be recapitulated, which is to say brought back into the wholeness of God in and through Christ the head, when God is "all in all" (1 Cor 15:28).

Tertullian (155–240 CE)

Tertullian is the first to use the language of "one substance *(substantia*[30]*)* in three persons *(personae)*"[31] arguing against modalism, a

[27] Ibid.

[28] Ibid., 168–69. Anatolios notes that this argument occurs in opposition to the gnostic worldview in which creation is the work of an evil god (168).

[29] Ibid.; cites AH 2.1.1–2.

[30] Note that modalism is saying that God is three only in modes of action, not in God's own being. Contemporary theologians such as Karl Rahner and Karl Barth are sometimes mistakenly portrayed as modalists, because they use the word *mode.* Rahner speaks of three modes of subsistence in the Trinity, and Barth speaks of three modes of existence in the Trinity. Both are saying that God has three modes of *being*, and therefore they are not modalists. The one God *exists* or *subsists* in three distinct ways or modes. In other words, the distinction is in God's very self, in God's being, not just in the way God acts in the world or the way God appears to us. Modalists say there is no distinction in God. The distinction is only in our perception or experience of God. Trinitarian theology says the distinction is in God. God is one *as* three.

[31] Marmion and Van Nieuwenhove, *An Introduction to the Trinity*, 61.

theory suggesting the One only appears to be three to us as opposed to being three in Godself. He is also the first to use the word *Trinity (Trinitas)*. The word *personae* or *prosopon* in the Greek had been used by the Sabellians (who were modalists) in its theatrical sense of mask to say that the one God puts on different faces or masks, appearing successively as the Father in creation, the Son in redemption, and the Spirit in sanctification. Tertullian, however, uses the term to emphasize a real distinction in God's own being. O'Collins elucidates:

> Where *substance* stood for the common fundamental reality shared by Father, Son, and Holy Spirit, Tertullian understood *person* as the principle of operative individuality. One could be led astray by the historical background of the Latin *persona* (and the Greek *prosopon*), as if the term meant only a mere mask or a mere manifestation. But Tertullian was no modalist monarchian when he wrote of the persons in God. At the same time, one must obviously beware of interpreting Tertullian in light of later, especially modern, theories of personhood, which expound persons as conscious selves and autonomous subjects.[32]

Tertullian maintains the distinction among the Three, but he is not proposing any type of separation between the Three that would make them three individual conscious and autonomous beings. He uses different images to convey this idea of distinction without separation between the Father and Son, such as thought or reason *(Ratio)* within God's mind and speech *(Sermo)* where the Father utters the Son/Word.[33] In Tertullian there is a difference between the Word within God's mind and the Word as it is expressed in creation. The Word is in God's mind as God's Wisdom, expressed in creation, and is only fully Son in the incarnation. For Tertullian, the immanent Word is not yet Son until the incarnation.

Prior to Tertullian, one God always referred to the Father. As we saw in Chapter 3, in continuity with the monotheistic tradition of Judaism, the one God is YHWH, whom Jesus and those who follow Jesus call Abba or Father. It is this God of Israel that raises Jesus

---

[32] O'Collins, *The Tripersonal God,* 105.

[33] Marmion and Van Nieuwenhove, *An Introduction to the Trinity*, 61; O'Collins, *The Tripersonal God*, 107.

from the dead and empowers him to send the Spirit. The Father is the source of the oneness and the divinity. In the East the Father is called the origin, font, and principle of divinity. In the West the Father is the *fons et origo plentitudinis divinitatis*, or the spring/fountain and origin/source of the plentitude of divinity. With Tertullian, the idea of "one God" takes on two meanings: the traditional meaning of God as Father in the economy (meaning God's plan of salvation in the created world) and the idea of the divine substance, the reality which stands under and is common to and shared in by the Father, Son, and Spirit.[34] All three share in the same one divine reality. Tertullian, like most of the early church fathers, is subordinationist, so the divinity underlies the three in different degrees, most fully in the Father and less so in the Son and Spirit.

After this distinction of the one God as the divine substance or Godhead that is shared by or common to the Three is made in Tertullian, a theory develops that the West begins trinitarian theology with the oneness of God and the East begins with the threeness of God, leading to modalistic dangers in the West and tritheistic dangers in the East. Contemporary scholarship in patristic trinitarian theology today debunks this so-called de Régnon paradigm (named after the theologian who first proposed the distinction).[35] Nonetheless, much of twentieth-century systematic theology uncritically repeats this paradigm, including authors such as Jürgen Moltmann, Colin Gunton,

---

[34] This point was made by Donald Buggert, O.Carm., in his lectures and course notes for "The Triune God" at Washington Theological Union, Washington DC (Spring 1999).

[35] This thesis was first seriously questioned by Michel Rene Barnes, "De Régnon Reconsidered," *Augustinian Studies* 26 (1995): 51–79. It has more recently been examined by Lewis Ayres, *Nicaea and Its Legacy* (Oxford: Oxford University Press, 2004). D. Glenn Butner offers a defense of de Régnon's paradigm within a limited context in "For and Against de Régnon," *International Journal of Systematic Theology* 17 (2015): 399–412. Coakley and Ayres also note the tendency to regard de Régnon's position in overly simplistic terms today. See Sarah Coakley, "Introduction: Disputed Questions in Patristic Trinitarianism," *Harvard Theological Review* 100, no. 2 (April 2007): 132; cites Ayres, *Nicaea and Its Legacy,* 413n56. Barnes himself credits Edmund Hill with first questioning this assumption in Karl Rahner's critique of Augustine's work *The Trinity*. See Edmund Hill, "Karl Rahner's Remarks on the Dogmatic Treatise *De Trinitate* and Saint Augustine," *Augustinian Studies* 2 (1977): 67–80.

and Cathrine Mowry LaCugna.[36] Sarah Coakley points out that theologians such as Vladimir Lossky, John Zizioulas, Miroslav Volf, and Colin Gunton have further used this false divide to make additional claims about difference between the East and the West on the Trinity regarding such matters as the role and consequence of mystery, relation, hierarchy, and individualism in this doctrine.[37]

Tertullian's famous analogies of the Trinity include a plant with its root, shoot, and fruit or a river with its fountain/spring, river, and streams or irrigation or canal. He also talks about the sun, its ray, and the point it touches the earth bringing forth life. These images are congruent with an image of the Source of Love enfolded and unfolding wholeness in the world. Notice in Tertullian's images that the Spirit has a role of bearing fruit or bringing forth life as it is to have in our lives.

Athanasius (297–371 CE)

Athanasius, as the great defender of the Council of Nicaea, argues that the Son is consubstantial with the Father, meaning the Son is of the same substance or one in being with the Father *(homoousios)*. He argues against Arius, who wants to say that the Son is created by the Father. For Arius, the Son is not a mere human being. He is created by the Father before all of creation, "the firstborn of all creation" (Col 1:15). Arius maintains that the Son is the agent of creation in that the Father creates the Son, who then creates everything else. Athanasius, who follows the scriptural notion that Jesus is the Wisdom of God, famously taunts Arius, asking, "When was God without his Wisdom?"[38] Athanasius is known for putting relationality at the

---

[36] Ayres, *Nicaea and Its Legacy*, 385n3; cited in Sarah Coakley, "Introduction: Disputed Questions in Patristic Trinitarianism," 131.

[37] Coakley, "Introduction: Disputed Questions in Patristic Trinitarianism," 131.

[38] Khaled Anatolios, "'When Was God without Wisdom?': Trinitarian Hermeneutics and Rhetorical Strategy in Athanasius," in *Studia Patristica* (Leuven: Peeters, 2006), 117–23. Anatolios notes that Athanasius is fully aware of the "two Wisdoms" theory of Arius, in which Arius holds for God's eternal wisdom but not the preexistent Christ.

center of the Trinity, using it to define both the distinction and the unity of the Trinity.[39] The Athanasian rule states: "The Father would not be Father without the Son, and that therefore the Father never was without the Son."[40] This idea is contrary to an earlier understanding in which the Word *becomes* Son in creation and redemption. As quoted in Chapter 1, Denis Edwards points out that for Athanasius, "God cannot be divided into parts, but the Son is whole from whole as eternal Image and Radiance of the Father."[41] Edwards highlights six images for the Trinity used by Athanasius in Paragraph 19 of his First Letter to Serapion: "1. Fountain, River, Spirit of Whom We Drink; 2. Light, Radiance, Illuminating Spirit; 3. Father, Son, Spirit Who Makes Us Sons and Daughters [Spirit of Adoption]; 4. Fountain of Wisdom, Wisdom of God, Gift of Wisdom; 5. Source of Life, Life, Life-Giving Spirit; 6. Father Works, Son Does the Works of the Father, the Works Are Accomplished in the Power of the Spirit."[42] As in Tertullian's trinitarian images, we see patterns in Athanasius's trinitarian images. The Father is the Source or Fountain. The Son is the revelation of the source. Edwards notes that the Father and Son are correlational; there is no Father without Son, no fountain/spring without the river, and no light without radiance. The Spirit acts to incorporate us into this relationship that is God. In other words, for Athanasius, the Spirit unites us to the Son, thus enabling us to partake in the relationship between the Son and the Father. As Edwards explains, "The whole argument is that the Spirit can enable our creaturely participation in God only if the Spirit is truly divine, and one with the Father and the Word."[43] Edwards cites Khaled Anatolios to describe this pattern of trinitarian images found in Athanasius: "In each case the Father is the source, the Son is the outgoing manifestation and imaged content of

---

[39] Veli-Matti Kärkkäinen, *The Trinity: Global Perspectives* (Louisville, KY: Westminster John Knox Press, 2007), 26.

[40] Ibid. Kärkkäinen adds that Origen had expressed this same idea earlier (26n27).

[41] Denis Edwards, "Athanasius' Letters to Serapion: Resource for a Twenty-First-Century Theology of God the Trinity," *Phronema* 29, no. 2 (2014): 45.

[42] Ibid., 48–49.

[43] Ibid., 50.

the source, and the Spirit is the outward actualization of that content in and towards creation."[44]

Khaled Anatolios makes a direct connection between Irenaeus's arguments for the Son and Spirit being part of God and Athanasius's arguments for the Son being consubstantial and the Spirit being divine. He notes that if the Son and the Spirit "are not God, then they are *in the way* of our immediate union with God."[45] In other words, if something other than God is mediating our relationship to God, we would not be in *immediate* union with God. Anatolios argues that for both Irenaeus and Athanasius, who God is in the economy must be who God is in Godself. The Son and the Spirit "must *be* God in order for the resultant relation between God and creation to *be* immediate."[46] In both, one also finds the connection between creation and incarnation. Humanity as dynamic receptivity is fulfilled and healed from the sin that has taken root in that receptivity "by the divine presence from within," which is to say, the incarnation and the Spirit's implanting that same Word made flesh into our hearts.[47]

Anatolios notes that the end point of this process of God's self-communication in Jesus is our divinization: "God became human that we might become divine."[48] Jesus as Son is a "Godward" God and thus "shares in and perfects humanity's Godward stance by being himself a divine exemplar of that stance."[49] At the same time he shows that both Irenaeus and Athanasius are not modalists and do preserve this distinction within God's own being. Without that distinction, we would lose our "Godwardness" and be absorbed into God.[50] Anatolios explains:

> But it is only through the differentiation by which Jesus is ultimately not simply God but the Godward God that the human

---

[44] Ibid.; cites Khaled Anatolios, *Retrieving Nicaea: The Development and Meaning of Trinitarian Doctrine* (Grand Rapids, MI: Baker Academic, 2011), 142–43.

[45] Anatolios, "The Immediately Triune God," 170; see also Khaled Anatolios, "The Influence of Irenaeus on Athanasius," in *Studia Patristica* (Louvain: Peeters, 2001): 463–76.

[46] Anatolios, "The Immediately Triune God," 159–78.

[47] Ibid., 170–71.

[48] Ibid., 172.

[49] Ibid.

[50] Ibid., 172–73.

> Godward stance can be immediately united to the divine Godward stance, while preserving the integrity of both God and humanity. . . . Our immediate union with the Incarnate Godward God is an immediate union with the God to whom he is toward, the Father.[51]

The Son is "toward the Father" both in Godself, the immanent Trinity, and as God for us, the economic Trinity, so that we can be incorporated into that same relationship. Anatolios uses language congruent with David Bohm's concept of enfolded wholeness, as was seen in Chapter 1. We have "a Godward God who enfolds humanity's Godward stance and brings it to its goal."[52]

The Spirit is then the one who unites Jesus to God and brings us into that union. The Son is the "Giver of the Spirit according to his divinity and yet the receiver of the Spirit in his humanity."[53] Anatolios adds:

> Building on the insights of these two early theologians [Irenaeus and Athanasius], we can say that if the Son is the Godward God, the Spirit is the one who actualizes the Godward stance of the Son as a human communal Godward stance. The Spirit is the one by whom the "I" of the Son's divine Godwardness becomes the "We" of humanity's communal Godwardness in the Son.[54]

He further explains:

> It is precisely because the Spirit is always the Spirit of Christ, the one who "adapts" the many members of the human race to the single normative stance of the Godward God, that this adaptation necessarily takes a communal form, for the Spirit brings together *(com-)* humanity into the *unity* of Christ. Both Irenaeus and Athanasius insist that Jesus's human reception of the Spirit constituted *our* reception of it (Irenaeus, AH III, 9, 3; Athanasius, CA 1:47). Thus, the point of the incarnation was not

---

[51] Ibid., 173.

[52] Ibid. Note that Anatolios uses this phrase to illustrate what is not possible under "Schleiermacher's reductive interpretation."

[53] Ibid., 176.

[54] Ibid.

> that the Godward stance of the divine Son may be enfleshed in a single individual, but that it may be distributed among humanity as a whole and gathered together into Jesus Christ.[55]

Anatolios explains more simply that the Spirit divinizes our human Godwardness by uniting it to the Son's divine Godwardness, stating that "we may then characterize the Spirit as, in a certain sense, the humanward God, who precisely as God, immediately effects the humanization of the Son's Godwardness that we may share in it."[56]

In all these activities, God is one. Edwards quotes Athanasius from *The First Letter to Serapion*:

> [The Trinity] is self-consistent and indivisible in nature, and it has one activity *(energeia)*. The Father does all things through the Word in the Holy Spirit. In this way is the unity of the Holy Trinity preserved, and in this way is the one God preached in the Church, "who is above all and through all and in all" (Eph 4:6)—"above all," as Father, as beginning *(archē)* and source; "through all," through the Word; "in all," in the Holy Spirit. It is not a Trinity in name alone and in linguistic expression, but in truth and actual existence.[57]

At the same time, while emphasizing the oneness of activity in the Trinity, Athanasius uses the same word, *energeia* (activity), to name the Spirit.[58] The Father always acts in the Spirit through the Word.[59] Athanasius, like those who went before him, tended more toward images of the Trinity rather than using a specific term to designate the Three. Edmund Fortman notes:

> He had no proper term for *person*, for he found both *prosopon* and *hypostasis* unsatisfactory. He regularly identified *ousia* and *hypostasis* (*De decret.* 27; *De syn.* 41; *Tom. Ad Ant.* 6); even as late as 369 he still wrote that "*hypostasis* is the same as *ousia*,

---

[55] Ibid.
[56] Ibid., 177.
[57] Edwards, "Athanasius' Letters to Serapion," 58; cites *Ser.* 1.28.2–3.
[58] Ibid., 60.
[59] Ibid.

> signifying nothing other than being itself" (*Ep. Ad Afr.* 4). But in the council of Alexandria in 362 he agreed that the formula "three hypostases" could be used legitimately to express the distinct subsistence of the three in the consubstantial Triad, provided that it did not carry the Arian connotation of three alien and separate substances (*Tom. Ad Ant.* 6).[60]

As was the case with Athanasius, until the fourth century *ousia* (substance or essence) and *hypostasis* (that which stands under or individualizes a substance) are used interchangeably to talk about the oneness of God. There is one substance, one essence, one *individual* in God. This oneness of God is emphasized to demonstrate that Christians are monotheists. As the focus turns to trying to understand the distinctness of the persons, particularly against those who are modalists (the Sabellians or the modalistic Monarchians), the Cappadocians and those following them use *hypostasis* to refer to what is distinct or unique or three in the Trinity, so God is referred to as having one *ousia* and three *hypostases*, one substance or essence that distinctly exists in three unique, individualized ways as Father, Son, and Spirit.[61] Basil states that "one who fails to confess the community of the essence or substance falls into polytheism, [and] the one who

---

[60] Edmund J. Fortman, *The Triune God: A Historical Study of the Doctrine of the Trinity* (Philadelphia: Westminster, 1972), 382.

[61] I am indebted to my professor, Donald Buggert, O.Carm., for the following breakdown and definition of these Greek terms, which the reader may find helpful: *Ousia*: What a thing is; its essence or mode of being, e.g., humanness, dogness: Ln *substantia/essentia* (substance/essence). In God, it would be God's "Godness" or divinity, that which is one or shared in the Trinity. *Hypostasis*: literally, that which stands under; the individualized or concrete instance of this or that *ousia*/substance, e.g., this human, this dog: Ln *subsistenia* (individual). (Note that at Nicaea *ousia* and *hypostasis* are used interchangeably so that Son is the same *hypostasis* and *ousia* as Father, emphasizing the oneness of God, that there is only one individual in God. Later trinitarian theology will say God is one *ousia* and three *hypostases* to emphasize the distinctness of the Three.) *Prosopon*: literally, mask or face; the reality as it appears to us or is manifest to us, what you see; the reality in its concrete properties (height, color, length): Ln *persona* (person). *Physis*: the principle/source of action or life in a reality; what makes a reality to act or live the way it does: also Ln *natura* (nature).

refuses to grant the distinction of the *hypostases* is carried away into Judaism (Letter 210.5)."[62]

The Cappadocians: Basil of Caesarea (330–79), Gregory Nazianzus (329–89), and Gregory of Nyssa (332–95)

Like Tertullian, the Cappadocians are concerned with defining orthodoxy against Sabellianism, the idea that Father, Son, and Spirit are simply roles played by the one God as opposed to real distinctions within God.[63] In a post-Nicene context they are also concerned with defending Nicaea against the Eunomians, who identified substance or *ousia* with being unbegotten, and so maintained that the Son, who is begotten, must be of a different substance from the Father.[64] Against the Sabellians and their use of *proposon* (person) in the theatrical sense of mask, the Cappadocians define *prosopon* as *hypostasis*, a word that had previously been identified with *ousia* or substance *(substantia)*.[65] Against the Eunomians, the Cappadocians make a strong distinction between substance and person, so that the substance of God is one and the Persons are defined by their unique properties of being unbegotten, begotten, and spirated.[66]

John Zizioulas explains the difference between nature/substance and person/hypostasis as the difference between *what* something is and *how* something is.[67] *What* God is, is one; *how* God is, is three. Zizioulas explains the Eastern concept of *theosis* or divinization in this way. We cannot become what God is, which is to say we cannot become God by nature, but we can come to be *how* God is.[68] In other words, *who* you become is more important than *what* you are; doing takes precedence over being. We can act in ways that are more

[62] Cited in Marmion and Van Nieuwenhove, *An Introduction to the Trinity*, 72.

[63] Jean Metr Zizioulas, "The Doctrine of the Holy Trinity: The Significance of the Cappadocian Contribution," in *Trinitarian Theology Today: Essays on Divine Being and Act*, ed. Christoph Schwöbel (Edinburgh: T & T Clark, 1995), 45–46.

[64] Ibid., 49.

[65] Ibid., 46–47.

[66] Ibid., 49–50.

[67] Ibid., 55.

[68] Ibid.

Godlike. To be true, authentic persons is to live out our humanity being more like God. The *how* of God is three, is relation. To be made in the image of God is to be made relational. The *what* and the *how* coincide in God as Love. God as Love generates the Son and spirates the Spirit. Love by nature is self-diffusive. Zizioulas argues:

> Love is not a feeling, a sentiment springing from nature like a flower from a tree. Love is a *relationship*, it is the free coming out of one's self, the breaking of one's will, a *free* submission to the will of another. It is the other and our relationship with him that gives us our identity, our otherness, making us "who we are," i.e. persons; for by being an inseparable part of a relationship that matters ontologically we emerge as *unique* and *irreplaceable* entities. This, therefore, is what accounts for our being, and our being ourselves and not someone else; our personhood. It is in this that the "reason," the *logos* of our being lies: in the relationship of love that makes us unique and irreplaceable *for another*.[69]

He adds:

> As a person you exist as long as you love and are loved. When you are treated as nature, as a thing, you die as a particular identity. And if your soul is immortal, what is the use? You will exist, but without a personal identity; you will be eternally dying in the hell of anonymity, in the Hades of immortal souls. For nature in itself cannot give you existence and being as an absolutely unique and particular identity. Nature always points to the general; it is the person that safeguards uniqueness and absolute particularity.[70]

To Zizioulas's perspective we can add the point that we learn *how* to be persons in and through the person of Jesus Christ, who is one in being or nature with God and one in being or nature with us. Jesus is unified in who he is (his person). What he is, his human nature and his divine nature, is unified in who he is (his person) in his loving and free relationships. This unity with the Father and this unity with us is

---

[69] Ibid., 56–57.

[70] Ibid., 57.

effected by the Holy Spirit. The Holy Spirit unites us and empowers us to be persons too. The Spirit does not change what we are (human, our nature) but changes *who* we are, *how* we live as persons.

One of the major contributions of Gregory Nazianzus to theology is the concept of perichoresis, discussed in Chapter 1. While initially used by Gregory Nazianzus to speak of the relationship among the human and divine natures in the person of Christ, the concept was later used to speak of the relationship between the three Persons of the Trinity.[71] Perichoresis is defined as interrelationship, mutual indwelling, coinherence, circumsession (from its Latin translation as the static *circumsessio*) or circumcession (from the active *circumcessio*).[72] While the term has been explained in more colloquial language as to dance around in/with one another, in which the dance cannot be separated from the dancers, this definition confuses the Greek *perichōreō* (to encompass) with *perichoreuō* (to dance around).[73] Verna Harrison suggests that Gregory of Nazianzus was drawing on the Stoic concept of mixture as "a complete mutual interpenetration of two substances that preserves the identity and properties of each intact."[74] The concept combines these ideas of complete mutual interpenetration and preservation of identity. The word also carries the connotations of both movement and rest. In terms of the Trinity, it is used to say that the Three exist in a relationship in which each encompasses the others (movement) and is encompassed by the others (rest). At the same time, the Three preserve their distinction from one another, their uniqueness and identity. This one Greek word, perichoresis, carries all of these meanings.

Perichoresis was further developed by Maximus the Confessor and then John of Damascus, through whom it found its way into Western theology as well. It is only in John of Damascus that we get the articulation of a comparison between the perichoresis of the two

---

[71] Daniel F. Stramara Jr., "Gregory of Nyssa's Terminology for Trinitarian Perichoresis," *Vigiliae Christianae* 52, no. 3 (1998): 258. See also Verna E. F. Harrison, "Perichoresis in the Greek Fathers," *St. Vladimir's Theological Quarterly* 35, no. 1 (1991): 55–56.

[72] Harrison, "Perichoresis in the Greek Fathers," 54.

[73] Catherine Mowry LaCugna, *God for Us: The Trinity and Christian Life* (San Francisco: HarperSanFrancisco, 1991), 312n94.

[74] Harrison, "Perichoresis in the Greek Fathers," 54.

natures of Christ and the perichoresis of the Persons of the Trinity.[75] Harrison concludes, "Despite its late appearance in the vocabulary of the fathers, perichoresis emerges as a key theological concept expressing the conjunction of unity and distinction, stability and dynamism, symmetry and asymmetry."[76] She goes on to suggest, in regard to its application to the Persons of the Trinity:

> This relationship among the persons is an eternal rest in each other but also an eternal movement of love, though without change or process. Gregory Nazianzus suggests the existence of such a dynamism, which need not in any way compromise the eternity and impassibility [un-change-ability] of God. The concept of perichoresis, at once static and dynamic, thus expresses the fact that in the relations of origin which constitute the Trinity, the hypostases are truly personal and God is truly love.

Maximus the Confessor (580–662 CE)

Nicholas Madden notes that Maximus the Confessor inherits his trinitarian terminology from the Cappadocian fathers and the councils.[77] By this time the Trinity had been defined as three *hypostases* and one nature *(physis)* or substance *(ousia)*. The names of Father, Son, and Spirit express the relations among the Three, not separate substances or natures. In other words, there is one God who is Father, Son, and Spirit. Madden explains what it means to say that the names are relations: "To call God the Father is not to say what he is, but to say what he is in relation to his Son."[78] The "Persons" are relations. The connectedness of the relation is what makes it what it is. The Father is not the Father without the Son. Madden adds that, for

---

[75] Ibid., 61.

[76] Ibid., 64.

[77] Nicholas Madden, "Maximus Confessor on the Holy Trinity and Deification," in *The Mystery of the Holy Trinity in the Fathers of the Church: The Proceedings of the Fourth International Patristic Conference* [Maynooth, 1999], ed. Vincent Twomey and Lewis Ayres (Portland, OR: Four Courts Press, 2007), 104.

[78] Ibid., 105.

Maximus, the relations "are replicated in the missions," meaning the incarnation for the Son, "and so in his flesh [the Son] manifests the Father and the Spirit."[79] What makes the Son the Son is the relatedness to the Father. This relationship is incarnate in Jesus of Nazareth. Who he *is* is relatedness to the Father. Who he *is* is the one who is filled with the Spirit. Thus who he *is* in the Trinity is who he *is* in the incarnation.

We cannot count or add up the Three so that God is the Father plus the Son plus the Spirit; rather, God exists in oneness as Three, a Three-ed One.[80] There is no chronological or hierarchical ordering to the Three. The One exists as Three. The Three are the realization of the One. Madden cites Maximus from the *Mystagogia* at length:

> God is One: one essence, three hypostases; One alone; as a substance of Three Hypostases, a consubstantial Trinity of Persons; only One in Trinity and a Trinity in Unity; not one unit plus another, nor one beside another, but the same Unity itself, in relation to, and for Itself; identical with itself, both a Unity and a Trinity, unconfused, holding to Its unity without confusion yet preserving its distinctions undivided and inseparable; a Unity with reference to what we call His Essence, that is to say His principle of being *(tou einai logos)* not through a synthesis, contraction or confusion of any kind; but still a Trinity in reference to the expression of His manner of existing or subsistence *(to pōs hyparchein kai huphestanai logos)* not however by division or alienation or separation of any kind. For the Persons cause no division in the Only One, nor is their Unity present, or considered to be present in them, in an incidental or merely relative way; neither are the Persons formed into a compound Unit, nor do they make it up by a process of contraction; the same hypostases or Persons is an unconfused Unity in essence and when considered simply in

---

[79] Ibid., 105–6.

[80] Ibid. Madden cites Maximus: "[The Triad] is not, as if by accomplishment of numerical diversity, a composition of monads presupposing division, but rather the monosubstantial (enousios) existence of the tri-hypostasised Monad (*1 Ambig.* PG 91, 1036B)." Madden goes on to explain, "The Monad [the One] is being but it exists as hypostases and this eternally; the Triad [the Three] is constituted by threefold hypostases but as the realisation of the existence of a substantial Monad, and this also in an eternal now" (106).

relation to Itself *(logos)*; in Its hypostases and the manner *(tropos)* of its existence the Holy Unity is a Trinity.[81]

All of which is to say, in the words of Zizioulas cited above, the nature or substance which is one is *what* God is. The three are *how* God is. Madden cites Maximus's conclusion about our knowledge of the Trinity, "For first we are illuminated with the reason for its being, then we are enlightened about the mode in which it subsists, for we always understand that something is before we understand how it is."[82] Thus, in the Threeness, God is one, and God's oneness or unity is manifested in God's threeness or as Trinity.[83] The oneness of the substance is the expression of the three in their distinctiveness. God is not Father *and* Son *and* Holy Spirit. God is one as Father, Son, Spirit. In God, oneness or unity *is* otherness or distinctiveness or diversity. God expresses Godself as plurality in otherness. As a model for us, we should not see otherness and diversity as a barrier to unity but rather as a prerequisite for unity. Unity is not a numerical compilation of more of the same. Unity is the communion of what is other. Recall John Haughey's point: "What does the Trinity do when it is off work? It ones."[84] Madden explains that, for Maximus, "it is their [the Persons'] nature to be united by the very constitution

---

[81] Madden, "Maximus Confessor on the Holy Trinity and Deification," 107; cites *Myst.* PG 91, 699D–701A, adding: "The translation is taken, with some modifications, from J. Stead, *The Church, the Liturgy, and the Soul of Man* (Still River, MA: St. Bede's Publications, 1982), 99–100.

[82] Madden, "Maximus Confessor on the Holy Trinity and Deification," 106; cites *1 Ambig.* PG 91, 1036C.

[83] Madden, "Maximus Confessor on the Holy Trinity and Deification," 107. Madden notes that Maximus excludes "quantity, contiguity, causality and emanation as ways of accounting for the distinctness of the hypostases, while synthesis, contraction and confusion are eliminated as ways of accounting for the *monas* [oneness]." Madden explains Maximus's phrase "*homoousia esti heterohypostasia*" (cites *Ep.* 15, PG 91, 549B) using an explanation by A. Nicholls: "The divine *homoousion*, as being common to the hypostases in their communion, is the direct and immediate expression of those Persons in their otherness" (cites A. Nicholls, *Byzantine Gospel* [Edinburgh: Bloomsbury T & T Clark, 1993], 80).

[84] John Haughey, *A Biography of the Spirit: There Lies the Dearest Freshness Deep Down Things* (Maryknoll, NY: Orbis Books, 2015), entry for Oct. 30.

of relationships."[85] The nature or substance of God is to be relation and otherness, in a word, Threeness. Thus the union of God's being *(ousia)* is the difference of the Three *(hypostases)*.[86] Madden notes that part of our human difficulty in understanding the Trinity is that we cannot understand "threeness without opposition of individuals," and we do not understand "unity that does not remove distinction."[87]

In Maximus we find a precursor and a ground for the foundational concepts in this book. Like Rahner, Maximus understands creation and incarnation to be two phases of the one plan of God for salvation. Like Jean-Luc Marion, Maximus envisions God as beyond even being, and thus uses love as the primary category for talking about God. Finally, like David Bohm and his concept of a reality of holons in which each part is in turn its own whole, Maximus understands each part of creation to be a whole in itself that, in turn, contains the whole. Maximus uses the concept of perichoresis to explain how each part encompasses and is encompassed by the whole, thus creating a web of interconnection at the heart of reality.

Maximus's trinitarian theology centers on the role of Christ in what Torstein Theodor Tollefsen calls a christocentric cosmology. Like Irenaeus before him and Rahner after him, Maximus understands creation to be for the sake of incarnation. Maximus speaks of three "incarnations" of Christ—in the cosmos, in scripture, and in the person of Jesus.[88] Tollefsen explains that for Maximus the incarnation is effected "always and in all" in and through the incarnation of *principles* in the cosmic order, *meaning* in the scriptures, and the *person* of Jesus the Christ.[89] Thus, for Maximus, the union of the human and divine in Christ is not "a single, contingent event in world history, but rather as 'that for which all things are ordained.'"[90]

According to Tollefsen, Maximus "thinks of the whole natural cosmos as made because of a Trinitarian motif, by the Son of God,

---

[85] Madden, "Maximus Confessor on the Holy Trinity and Deification," 112.

[86] Ibid.

[87] Ibid.

[88] Torstein Tollefsen, "Christocentric Cosmology," in *The Oxford Handbook of Maximus the Confessor*, ed. Pauline Allen and Bronwen Neil (Oxford: Oxford University Press, 2015), 308.

[89] Ibid.

[90] Ibid.; cites Carl Laga and Carlos Steel, *Maximus Confessor: Quaestiones ad Thalassium II* (Turnhout: Brepols, 1990), 75.

with him as the centre of all created being, and with a view to the establishment of communion between created and uncreated being in Christ."[91] Tollefsen explains, "The term 'Christocentric cosmology' is meant to indicate that the whole history of the cosmos, of its beginning and end, and of its ontological constitution and purpose has its centre in Christ, the Logos of God. This conception of the cosmos comprises therefore both Creation and salvation, conceived of as two phases of the one divine Economy."[92] Maximus uses the image of a circle to express this christocentric cosmology. The Logos is the center of the circle and the source of creation, which comes forth from the center like the radii of the circle.[93]

For Maximus, we participate in the Logos because we are created in and through the Logos. Maximus is drawing on the scriptural images of John 1:3, that through the Word all things came to be, and Colossians 1:15–17, in which Christ is described as the agent of creation in whom and through whom and for whom all things were made.[94] The circumference of the circle is then that which unifies all creation and brings it back to created cosmos. Tollefsen explains, "Beings come forth from God and shall convert to God. The final purpose of the whole of being is a state of consummation or transfiguration. In the fulfillment of this purpose the effects of the hypostatic union are actualized in the deification of human beings and the cosmos, each in accordance with their fitness for achievement."[95] In other words, the circumference of the circle indicates that we not only come from God, we also return to God. God encompasses us. The cosmos is created

---

91 Torstein Tollefsen, *The Christocentric Cosmology of St. Maximus the Confessor* (Oxford: Oxford University Press, 2008), 1.

92 Tollefsen, "Christocentric Cosmology," 307.

93 Ibid.

94 Ibid., 314.

95 Ibid., 311; cites Tollefsen, *The Christocentric Cosmology of St. Maximus the Confessor*, 185–86, 217–18. Tollefsen summarizes, "Christ is the centre from which the principles of beings . . . stretch forth like radii. These are kept within the circumference that circumscribes their extremity and are brought back to God like straight lines fastened to the centre. . . . Divine Providence secures the being of beings by circumscribing them and protecting them from falling into non-being. Beings are secured, however, not just in the order of nature, but rather with a view to the consummation of beings in their transformation. The focus is therefore soteriological as well as cosmological. Christ is at the centre of the natural cosmos" (311).

in Christ. All creation is unified with God in the incarnation so that we might return to God through our own deification. What Christ is by nature, we are by adoption. Deification does not mean we become God. It means we become Godlike. We do not become *what* God is. We become *how* God is.

This image of the circle is also connected to Maximus's notion of wholeness: "This idea of the Logos as source finds its expression in the image of the circle, its centre, radii, and circumference, in a striking conception of the world as a whole, comprising parts that also are wholes comprising further parts—parts mirror the wholes and vice versa."[96] As Tollefsen explains, "Each part of a whole is wholly what the whole is, while at the same time differs from other parts of the same whole."[97] Tollefsen summarizes Maximus's idea of the wholeness of creation:

> This 'whole' is constituted by an orderly arrangement imposed by God on the parts. . . . Only in light of this whole are the parts adequately understood, because the whole reveals the parts in the divine scheme of things, in the *oikonomia* of the created cosmos. . . . The one Logos of God the Father gathers this totality together into unity. The collection is illustrated by the image of the circle, its centre and radii. . . . The principle, which is God comprising the collection of divine Ideas, *transcends* the world, but is at the same time somehow at work *immanently* in it.[98]

In Maximus's vision "the transcendent God is the unifying power in the cosmos and keeps beings in a well-ordered system of unity in plurality. The church, likewise, unifies people who differ in all kinds of aspects and makes them one as being baptized into Christ."[99] Like the image of the Trinity found in Maximus, the church as body of Christ ideally should be able to hold "diversity without opposition" and "unity that does not remove distinction."[100] Such community is only possible when the Spirit unites the body of Christ.

---

[96] Tollefsen, "Christocentric Cosmology," 308.

[97] Ibid., 317.

[98] Tollefsen, *The Christocentric Cosmology of St. Maximus the Confessor*, 50.

[99] Tollefsen, "Christocentric Cosmology," 310, 311.

[100] Madden, "Maximus Confessor on the Holy Trinity and Deification," 103.

While Maximus's cosmology holds Christ as the source and goal of creation, he also advocates a radical dissimilarity between God and creation, so that "in effect he argues that if God is being, beings *are* not, and if beings are, God *is* not."[101] Gale Woloschak contends:

> Maximus argues that all of creation has its grounding in nonbeing, and thus the only division between being and nonbeing is based in the Creator who is able to create out of nothing and who is both Being and Nonbeing in One, Christ the Logos. By the term nonbeing here, Maximus is using an apophatic approach to explain what cannot be explained literally much like Dionysius the Areopagite (or Denys as he is often called); and what he means by nonbeing is actually 'beyond being' and thus referring to the Creator.[102]

In a position that anticipates that of Jean-Luc Marion, Maximus says God is beyond being in that "the being of God has no contrary, not even non-being (cf. *Car.* 3.27–8)."[103] Creation, however, "was brought from non-being to being by God. . . . Beings are kept in being by absolute dependence on the power of God. Separated from Him their being will dissolve into non-being."[104] In other words, God is beyond even our categories of being and nonbeing. As Jean-Luc Marion argues, we are contingent on being. God is not. Being may be the most central category for us—to exist or not to exist. Being, however, is not the most central category for God. God is more than

---

[101] Tollefsen, "Christocentric Cosmology," 309.

[102] Gayle E. Woloschak, "The Broad Science-Religion Dialogue: Maximus, Augustine, and Others," in *Science and the Eastern Orthodox Church*, ed. Daniel Buxhoeveden and Gayle Woloschak (Farnham, Surrey, England: Ashgate, 2011), 138; cites Lars Thunberg, *Microcosm and Mediator: The Theological Anthropology of Maximus the Confessor*, 2nd ed. (Chicago: Open Court, 1995), 401, and Paul M. Blowers, *Maximus the Confessor: Jesus Christ and the Transfiguration of the World* (Oxford: Oxford University Press, 2016), 56. An apophatic approach is one that says what God is *not* rather than what God is, acknowledging that God is ultimately mystery and all of our words and concepts fall short.

[103] Tollefsen, "Christocentric Cosmology," 310–11; cf. Jean-Luc Marion, *God without Being: Hors-Texte,* trans. Thomas A. Carlson, 2nd ed. (Chicago: University of Chicago Press, 2012).

[104] Tollefsen, *The Christocentric Cosmology of St. Maximus the Confessor*, 55.

Being. God brings being or existence out of nothing; therefore God is beyond even Being itself.

Maximus sees love rather than being as the primary category for understanding God, particularly understanding God in relation to God's creation. Love is the source of all being. Love is the purpose of creation. Tollefsen explains:

> The divine economy comprises both creation and salvation. In fact, creation and salvation are two stages in one and the same divine purpose: to make beings and unite them with God. Beings are made with a view to deification. In this we perceive how the central motif of the Maximian system is the divine *philanthropia* [love of humanity], the great mystery that transcends all thought. . . . The divine love is the essential mystery of Christianity. . . . The most profound meaning of the cosmos, its purpose and inner structures is situated in the triadic being of God, with Christ the Logos as centre of it all.[105]

God is Love, and that Love is expressed and revealed in the incarnation. Madden notes, "[Love] is given as the ultimate reason for the hypostatic union on which depends the whole possibility of the manifestation of the Trinity implied in *deiknus* [bring to light, to show forth], a showing to enable us to realize the implications of the mystery into which we have been drawn by the love of God."[106] Love is the key to the incarnation in which the Logos draws humanity into the Trinity.

Madden explains that, for Maximus, "the fact of Jesus is a revelation of the divine philanthropy."[107] Jesus reveals God as Love. To experience the person of Jesus is to experience being in communion with the Father and the Spirit.[108] In the union of the divinity and humanity in the person of Jesus we are brought into the Trinity to experience the God who is Love as Source, Word, and Spirit.

---

105 Ibid.

106 Madden, "Maximus Confessor on the Holy Trinity and Deification," 103.

107 Ibid., 101.

108 Ibid., 106.

Jesus as the Word made flesh reveals the Father through his intelligence *(ennous)* connected to the Father as mind *(nous)* and the Spirit through his life *(zōn)* connected to the Spirit as life *(zōē)*.[109] Maximus thus relates the Trinity to the incarnation, because, for Maximus, "The Father, designated as *Nous*, is the generator of the Logos and the source of Life *(Zōē)*."[110] Thus we become "sons in the Son," and we share in the divine life, also becoming intelligent *(ennous)* and alive *(zōn)* like Christ through the love of God.[111]

This participation in the Trinity is lived out in one's life as love, *agape*. Madden notes:

> The reign of *agapē* in human life has profound significance for Maximus as it is the grace of filiation and so brings about a participation in the Son's relation to the Father, which is synonymous with his being Son and releases man into a fullness of life—*zōē*. This is the work of the Spirit. It is easy to conclude that theosis is from the Father in the Son and by the Spirit. . . . The ripening of this life produces a person in the true sense, so that as Maximus sees it, human *tropos hyparxeōs* or *tropos tou pōs einai* [roughly, the way a person is or how a person is] is the masterpiece of the Spirit's work, a condition that brings man within the mystery of the divine life and makes him a 'sharer in the divine nature'.[112]

When we live out love, we are sons and daughters of God, participating in the very life of the Trinity and becoming more like God, and thus more fully and authentically human, as humans were created to be. Madden explains, "We glorify the *Logos* when our lives are resplendent with the impress of their source, when our conduct shows

---

[109] Ibid. Note that unlike some of the earlier fathers and Greek philosophy that identified Nous with Logos as the Son distinct from the Father as the One, Maximus distinguishes between Nous (mind) as the Father and Logos (reason) as the Son.

[110] Ibid., 112.

[111] Ibid., 108–9.

[112] Ibid. *Tropos hyparxeōs* is the way/manner/mode of existence/being and *tropos tou pōs einai* is the way/manner/mode that it is or mode of how it is.

that we are God's children 'by what we think or do.'"[113] We find our personhood in the person of Christ, but this process is always trinitarian in structure. Madden explains: "It is by participation in the grace of the Spirit that we become *koinōnoi* of the divine nature, that is, personal participants in that nature through synergy with the Spirit, with whose freedom we interlock in becoming persons through his anointing of our being with his *agape*. It is as persons that we are sons, and it is the Son who compasses this through the action of the Spirit."[114] Madden summarizes Maximus's position: "Christ is the source of man's being, the fullness of life which the Holy Spirit poured into man, pours into him as *agape*, and which stabilizes him in God the Father because of his being identified with the eternal Son."[115] That *agape* is lived out as "the mutually reinforcing mode of love" of God and neighbor, in which "without love for God, one cannot truly love the neighbor, and without love for neighbor, one cannot truly love God."[116] This process of becoming sons in the Son by the power of the Spirit is the process of deification, which again is not to say that one becomes God, but rather one becomes Godlike or Christlike. In the Eastern tradition this process has been understood as the restoration of our likeness to God that was lost in the fall.

Maximus connects his idea of deification with the concept of perichoresis, describing revelation as the perichoresis of the believer with the object of belief.[117] Maximus speaks of perichoresis in both the case

[113] Ibid., 113. Madden adds, "We are related to the Logos who is *ennous* [intelligent] and *zōn* [alive] by being caught into his personal relation to his Father, able to say Abba, not by mimicry but out of an ontological transformation that makes us children in name and in truth, a condition identical with being a person in this view of things" (113).

[114] Ibid.

[115] Ibid., 117.

[116] Susan Wessel, "The Theology of Agape in Maximus the Confessor," *St. Vladimir's Quarterly* 55, no. 3 (2011): 322.

[117] Harrison, "Perichoresis in the Greek Fathers," 58. Verna Harrison suggests that for Maximus, perichoresis "appears to characterize reality at every level"—as part of the structure of the natural world, as the relationship between God and divinized creation, and in the hypostatic union of Christ between Creator and creation. She goes on to state, "If coinherence *(perichōrēsis)* truly characterizes every level of reality, it must occur first among the persons of the Trinity" (59). Maximus himself, however, never makes this leap, using perichoresis purely in a christological and anthropological sense.

of the incarnation and in the process of deification of the Christian believer. In that process of deification the believer participates in the whole, and to use David Bohm's language, becomes a subwhole in which the enfolded wholeness of God, in whose image and likeness we are created, is unfolded in the world through the deified person.

In this vision, which is remarkably similar to the Bohmian analogy suggested earlier in this work, God is the enfolded whole that unfolds itself in creation in and through the interconnection of all that exists, so that each part enfolds the whole, and in doing so, enfolds every other part. Harrison suggests that the concept of perichoresis can express the relationship between and among God and the created world. Harrison concludes:

> In regard to the created world, Maximus's understanding of perichoresis is particularly suggestive. He sees it first of all as a kind of interconnectedness and commingling among created things themselves. Added to this is the mutual indwelling of God and the saints, who, in an ever-active repose that is both static and dynamic, become identical to him in energy as far as is possible. By extension, life in the Kingdom can perhaps be envisaged as a mutual interchange of energies, i.e., of the free and conscious personal life and self-manifestation of all who participate in it. There is, in other words, a radical giving of one's own being to God and to all other persons, as far as is possible, and a receiving of theirs in return. This perichoresis of love is the created likeness and manifestation of the Holy Trinity, and it ultimately extends through glorified angelic and human persons to include all varieties of created beings in a coinherence with God and with each other.[118]

Thus Harrison is able to suggest that "perichoresis, which genuinely unites while preserving distinctness and enables mutuality and interchange of life itself among radically unequal levels of reality, thus stands at the heart of a Christian ontology of love."[119]

---

[118] Ibid., 65.
[119] Ibid.

Chapter 5

The Trinitarian Theology of Karl Rahner

The Jesuit theologian Karl Rahner was part of a twentieth-century theological movement often referred to as Transcendental Thomism. Theologians in this era were trained in the Scholastic theology of Thomas Aquinas. Rahner and other Transcendental Thomists then took the Thomistic theology of the Catholic tradition and put it into dialogue with the philosophy of Kant, Hegel, and Heidegger, among others. The result was a move called the turn to the subject or the anthropocentric (literally human-centered) turn, in which the focus became the experience of the human person or subject. Rather than beginning the theological endeavor with divinely revealed truths, either from scripture or tradition, the Transcendental Thomists began with the human experience of transcendence or openness to the transcendent.

Humans as Created for God

To transcend something is to move beyond it. Human experience, they suggest, always implies an openness to something beyond us. We experience this openness to the beyond by the fact that no finite event or object ever satisfies us. We always move beyond. Every answer leads us to a new question. We always move toward the something more. We transcend every finite event or object. We experience our unlimitedness in the fact that we chafe at our limits. In recognizing our limits we have already moved beyond them, which is to say we have transcended them. We experience this transcendence in the concrete reality of our lives.

We put all of our effort into achieving a goal, such as finishing school, but then we graduate and move beyond school to focus on our career or relationships or family or some combination of those factors. Some people get to a point in their lives where they decide to have children, but those children grow up and move on. Ultimately, we must continue to seek new experiences and new relationships of love, friendship, and service to create meaning in our lives. Many will continue to experience a certain restlessness even in the midst of deeply meaningful lives. Many will seek to satiate that restlessness with the things of this world, power and money, or even relationships of love and service. Nothing kills a relationship faster than trying to make another person be God for you. Rahner suggests that if we try to fill that space in us with what is not God, we will ultimately feel dissatisfied.

Rahner called this openness in the human person the *capax infiniti* or *capax Dei* (the capacity for the infinite or the capacity for God). The "more" toward which we move is God. We were created with this openness, this God-sized hole in our hearts, because we were created to be in relationship with God. As Augustine famously states: "You created us for yourself, O Lord, and our heart is restless until it rests in thee."[1] We experience this capacity for God in the inability of any finite thing to satisfy us.

Rahner notes that some would suggest that just because we experience this openness and dynamism does not necessarily imply that we are moving toward something. In our reaching out, in our openness, we experience emptiness, fragility as well as hope, freedom, and responsibility. We ultimately must make a choice. Do we believe our transcendence is grounded in nothingness and absurdity or in absolute meaning? Perhaps this experience of movement is just an absurdity of human nature, a cosmic joke. Perhaps what we are moving toward is nothingness. Rahner would agree that naming the term of our movement *God* is to take a leap of faith. He is not offering a proof for the existence of God. He is, however, asking us to examine our own experience. Can nothingness ground our lives? How can nothingness be what draws us and moves us? Rahner suggests that it cannot.

---

[1] Saint Augustine, *Confessions*, ed. Henry Chadwick (Oxford: Oxford University Press, 2008; 1992), 3.

God as Mystery of Love

If we believe that our lives are ultimately meaningful, then we must believe that our openness, dynamism, and movement are grounded in something bigger, something more. Rahner argues that God is the infinite mystery that cannot be transcended—that which we cannot move beyond. God is the horizon of our movement, that which both grounds our movement as its source and is the term of our movement, that which we move toward. God is the reality beneath and beyond all things. And thus, for Rahner, we co-experience or co-know God in every experience of our lives. Rahner calls this co-experience of God *Vorgriff*, literally "pre-grasp," but a difficult word to translate. This "knowledge" is not cognitive knowledge but affective knowledge, not head knowledge but heart knowledge.[2] We "know" God by heart.

So who or what is this "God" who grounds our transcendence and gives our lives absolute meaning? Rahner suggests the word *God* is not an object to be defined but rather a question we ask about the totality of our existence. Asking this question is part of what it means to be human. The word itself, *God,* tells us nothing of who God is. It functions like a name with no reference to an experience outside of the word itself (unlike the word *Father*, which we understand based on our experience of human fathers). Rahner states:

> For it is itself the final word before wordless and worshipful silence in the face of the ineffable mystery. It is the word which must be spoken at the conclusion of all speaking if, instead of silence in worship, there is not to follow that death in which man becomes a resourceful animal or a sinner lost forever. It is an almost ridiculously exhausting and demanding word. If we were not hearing it this way, then we would be hearing it as a word about something obvious and comprehensible in everyday life, as a word alongside other words. Then we would have heard something which has nothing in common with the true word "God" but its phonetic sound.[3]

---

[2] See Heidi Russell, *The Heart of Rahner: The Theological Implications of Andrew Tallon's Theory of Triune Consciousness*, vol. 64 (Milwaukee, WI: Marquette University Press, 2009).

[3] Karl Rahner, *Foundations of Christian Faith: An Introduction to the Idea of Christianity*, trans. William Dych (New York: Crossroad, 1978), 51.

In other words, the word *God* encompasses our relationship to the infinite and incomprehensible mystery that grounds our very being. For Rahner this God is the source and horizon of all being, of all existence. When one experiences and surrenders to this mystery, one discovers that it is the mystery and source of all love.

Thus, for Rahner, we cannot come to know God as we know an object or even another person. Our knowledge of God is unthematic and unreflexive, meaning that it is something that is deeper than thoughts and words. All thoughts and words we use to articulate that experience are secondary and fall short of the experience itself. Rahner says, "The concept 'God' is not a grasp of God by which a person masters the mystery, but it is letting oneself be grasped by the mystery which is present and yet ever distant. This mystery remains a mystery even though it reveals itself to man and thus continually grounds the possibility of man's being subject."[4] We can only know and experience God in and through our encounter with the world and other people. We do not directly experience God. God is co-experienced and co-known in and through every experience we have.

Rahner maintains that our primary experiences of God are through our own experience of self-actualization and love of neighbor. In other words, we experience God in and through our becoming persons like Jesus the Christ and in and through our relationships of community empowered by love in the Spirit. Rahner notes that from our side of the equation, our relationship with God is like that to the horizon or like the image of an asymptote. One moves toward a horizon but never arrives. The horizon recedes as one approaches. And yet it is the horizon that makes it possible to encounter and grasp finite objects. In our own terms we might also say that God is the wholeness. We do not see the wholeness, but each and every experience we have occurs against the backdrop of wholeness. We see objects in the foreground against a background. We often do not see the background. Imagine driving on a cloudy day, the sun hidden behind the clouds. The light enables you to see trees, houses, the road, but you do not see the light. The light is what enables you to see. You are co-experiencing and co-knowing the light with every object that you see.

A favorite image of Rahner's is the geometrical concept of an asymptote. An asymptote is a curve and a line that approach one another, in which you can divide the space between the two lines in half.

[4] Ibid., 54.

You can then divide that space in half again, and again, and again, on to infinity, and the two lines will never meet. Similarly Rahner uses the image of the asymptote to show us moving closer to God while at the same time showing that we can never reach God. God is always still infinitely far away from us. The image suggests that by our own efforts, we cannot reach God. The good news of the gospel is that we do not have to reach God, because God has reached us. God draws near to us. God draws near to us in what theologians call the economy of salvation (meaning God's plan and acts of salvation) through the Son and Spirit. God reveals Godself to us in the Son and the Spirit.

Rahner famously complains that "despite their orthodox confession of the Trinity, Christians are, in their practical life, almost mere 'monotheists.' We must be willing to admit, that should the doctrine of the Trinity have to be dropped as false, the major part of religious literature could well remain virtually unchanged."[5] Many people dismiss the Trinity as something beyond comprehension and therefore spend little time thinking about why the fact we believe our God to be triune might be significant to who we are as human beings.

For Rahner, to speak of God is to speak of God the Father. There is no generic God we can speak of apart from the Trinity. Rahner argues that such a position is not Latin or Greek, it is biblical.[6] Following Irenaeus, Rahner suggests that God the Father reveals Godself to us in the Son and the Spirit. He argues against a traditional (sometimes called Latin) way of talking about the Godhead or God's oneness apart from talking about God as Trinity, Father, Son, and Spirit. As a result, God or the Godhead almost becomes a fourth person of the Trinity, so that we talk about God in addition to the Father, the Son, and the Spirit. Rahner suggests instead that to use the term *God* is to refer biblically to the Unoriginate Source of the Trinity, God the "Father." Rahner explains: "Here God is the 'Father,' that is, the simply unoriginated God, who is always known as presupposed, who communicates himself precisely when and because his self-communication does not simply coincide with him in lifeless identity. In this self-communication he stays the one who is free, incomprehensible—in a word, unoriginated."[7] Rahner suggests

---

[5] Karl Rahner, *The Trinity*, trans. Joseph Donceel (New York: Crossroad Publishing, 1997), 10–11.

[6] Ibid., 83–84.

[7] Ibid., 84.

that we might talk about three "distinct manners of subsisting" in the Trinity and that "the first manner of subsisting at once constitutes God as Father, as unoriginated principle of divine self-communication and self-mediation. Hence no 'God' should be conceived behind this first manner of subsisting, as previous to this distinct subsistence and having first to assume it."[8] In other words there is not first God, who then subsists in three different manners (such would be modalism), but rather God *is* the distinct manners of subsisting. God *is* Father begetting the Son and spirating the Spirit. Rahner adds that "the expression 'distinct manners of subsisting' has the advantage of not as easily insinuating as 'three persons' the multiplication of the essence and of the subjectivity."[9] While many hear the word *person* as meaning a center of activity, subjectivity, and liberty, Rahner argues:

> But there are not three of these in God—not only because in God there is only *one* essence, hence *one* absolute self-presence, but also because there is only *one* self-utterance of the Father, the Logos. The Logos is not the one who utters, but the one who is uttered. And there is properly no *mutual* love between Father and Son, for this would presuppose two acts. But there is loving self-acceptance of the Father (and of the Son, because of the [order] of knowledge and love), and this self-acceptance gives rise to the distinction. . . . But there are not three consciousnesses; rather, the one consciousness subsists in a threefold way.[10]

In other words, the phrase *manner of subsisting* is less prone to tritheistic interpretations that result in a conception of Trinity as three individuals than is the word *person.* Admittedly, however, the phrase *manner of subsisting* is a bit harder to relate to on a personal and spiritual level.

The Economic Trinity and the Immanent Trinity

One of Rahner's most famous axioms is: *"The 'economic' Trinity is the 'immanent' Trinity and the 'immanent' Trinity is the 'economic'*

---

[8] Ibid., 112.

[9] Ibid., 113.

[10] Ibid., 106–7.

Trinity."[11] The economic Trinity is God as God has revealed Godself in the plan of creation and redemption, which is often referred to as the economy of salvation, hence the name economic Trinity. The economic Trinity is God as God is for us *(pro nobis)*. The immanent Trinity refers to who God is in Godself or God *in se*. Rahner's core concept is the idea of God's self-communication, which is to say that God has revealed God's very self in the Son and Spirit. What we have in the incarnation of the Son and the gift of the Holy Spirit in grace is not simply a communication *about* God; rather, it is God giving God's own self to us, to creation. Thus what we experience of God in the economic Trinity *is* who God is in Godself, which is the immanent Trinity. The fact that it is the Logos who is incarnate and the Spirit who descends upon us reveals something about the Trinity to us that is true not only of the "economic missions" (the way God acts in the world), but is true of the immanent Trinity itself.[12] Who God is for us is who God is in Godself because God has given God's very self to us.

Rahner maintains that our knowledge of the Trinity comes not just from the revelation of scripture but from the self-communication of God. He states: "The Trinity is not for us a reality which can only be expressed as a doctrine. The Trinity itself is with us, it is not merely given to us because revelation offers us statements about it. Rather these statements are made to us because the reality of which they speak is bestowed upon *us*."[13] While God's self-communication does reveal to us the God who is incomprehensible mystery, it would be a mistake to think the doctrine of the Trinity is something to which we profess belief but should not try to understand or appropriate. Rahner suggests that we try to escape this mystery by accumulating more concepts and distinctions to explain it "which operate as tranquilizers for *naïvely* shrewd minds, and dull the pain they feel when they have to worship mystery without understanding it."[14] Rather, Rahner

---

[11] Ibid., 22. Note that this axiom has led to considerable debate in the theological community. See Dennis W. Jowers, *The Trinitarian Axiom of Karl Rahner: The Economic Trinity Is the Immanent Trinity and Vice Versa* (Lewiston, NY: Edwin Mellen Press, 2006); Randal Rauser, "Rahner's Rule: An Emperor without Clothes?" *International Journal of Systematic Theology* 7, no. 1 (2005): 81–94.

[12] Rahner, *The Trinity*, 85–87.

[13] Ibid., 39.

[14] Ibid., 47.

suggests that "we can really grasp the content of the doctrine of the Trinity only by going back to the history of salvation and grace, to our experience of Jesus and of the Spirit of God who operates in us, because in them, we really already possess the Trinity itself as such."[15] We experience God as mystery, but we experience God. God has given Godself to us. Rahner points out that when we speak of the mystery and incomprehensibility of God:

> It does not mean only or mainly that this mystery consists in the special logical difficulty we experience in putting together the concepts used to express it. It means rather that this mystery is essentially identical with the mystery of the self-communication of God to us in Christ and in his Spirit. . . . The Father is the incomprehensible origin and the original unity, the "Word" his utterance into history, and the "Spirit" the opening up of history into the immediacy of its fatherly origin and end. And precisely this Trinity of salvation history, as it reveals itself to us by deeds, is the "immanent" Trinity.[16]

Likewise, then, anything we say about the immanent Trinity or who God is in Godself, must be grounded in the economic Trinity. Our doctrines of the Trinity must be grounded in who God has revealed Godself to be in the incarnation of Christ and gift of the Holy Spirit.

Rahner explains that God's self-communication "reveals to us a four-fold group of aspects: (a) Origin-Future; (b) History-Transcendence; (c) Invitation-Acceptance; (d) Knowledge-Love."[17] In other words, in Christ we experience God as origin, history, invitation, and knowledge. In the Spirit we experience God as future, transcendence, acceptance, and love. He further explains the double nature of these aspects in that

> when God's self-communication as beginning and history is still given as offer, it also appears as faithful truth, and it turns into history. This revelation of God in history, the offer or invitation made to us, is the incarnation in Jesus Christ. We experience God as Truth in this inbreaking of God into our history. Yet,

---

[15] Ibid., 40.
[16] Ibid., 46–47.
[17] Ibid., 88.

> as such, it is not yet *the* promise which has already penetrated into the addressee, has been accepted by him, *becoming* love and *begetting* love in him.[18]

This inbreaking of God into history is not yet God active in me personally. The divine self-communication has two modalities, truth and love. These two modalities "constitute the one divine self-communication which assumes the form of truth in history, of origin and offer, of love in transcendence towards the freely accepted absolute future."[19] I have to accept that offer and invitation, and I can only do so in and through the Spirit. I can only do so in and through love. Rahner explains that "both basic modalities condition one another. They derive from the nature of the self-communication of the unoriginated God who remains incomprehensible, whose self-communication remains a mystery both as possible and as actual. But the two modalities are not simply the same thing."[20] In my life God the Source of Love remains an incomprehensible mystery, but that Love is revealed as a possibility in Jesus Christ and can be made actual in my life through the Holy Spirit.

The Self-Express-Ability of God

God has two possibilities of being God for us, in the Logos and the Spirit. The Logos or Word of God is the eternal self-expression and therefore "self-express-ability" of God. The Word is always the Word *of God the Father*. God the Father's Word is spoken into the world. If God is going to reveal Godself to us, God speaks the Word. The Word is the ability in God to become what is not God, namely human. God expresses that self-express-ability in the incarnation. This is why only the Logos becomes incarnate. As the self-expression of God within the Trinity, the Logos is also the possibility of God expressing Godself outward. There is a congruence between who God is in Godself and who God is for us, the immanent Trinity and the economic Trinity.

Rahner argues that it must be the Logos that becomes incarnate, even if the incarnation is effected by the Trinity as a whole.[21] God

[18] Ibid., 96.
[19] Ibid., 98.
[20] Ibid., 99.
[21] Ibid., 23.

always acts as one. In all actions of the Trinity, it is always God the Father acting through the Son/Word by the power of the Spirit. Rahner explains that in the self-communication of God, "the Father gives himself to us too as *Father*, that is, precisely because and insofar as he himself, being essentially with *himself*, utters himself and *in this way* communicates the Son as his own, personal self-manifestation."[22] In our experience of God incarnate in Christ the Son and by the power of the Spirit who makes us sons and daughters in the Son, God reveals Godself to be our Father, our Abba. The Father gives *himself* to us *as Father* in the incarnation. The Son is the revelation of our Father, our Abba, to us. Rahner argues that the Father who is Unoriginate and invisible reveals by sending the Word, noting that "a revelation of the Father without the Logos and his incarnation would be like speaking without words."[23] God speaks God's Word to us in the incarnation of Jesus Christ.

Jesus is the sacrament of God. The human nature of Jesus is the visible sacrament that makes the Logos visible. The Logos is the self-expression of God, both in the immanent Trinity or in God's own self, and in the economic Trinity in the incarnation. If Jesus is to be the self-expression of God as the incarnate Logos, then Jesus's human life must somehow also be the life of the Logos expressing itself. Rahner acknowledges that point, stating that "the Logos of God himself establishes this corporeal part of the world as his own reality, both creating and accepting it at the same time. Hence he establishes it as what is different from himself in such a way that this very materiality expresses *him*, the Logos himself, and allows him to be present in his world."[24]

Rahner sees the world as created for the purpose of incarnation. God creates what is other than God in order to be in union with it. Rahner explains that creation is a moment within God's self-communication, created as "the condition of the possibility of constituting an

[22] Ibid., 35.

[23] Ibid., 29.

[24] Rahner, *Foundations of Christian Faith*, 196–97. It should be noted that it would be more appropriate to speak of God as establishing and creating the human reality, and God through the Logos assuming that human reality, but the point still remains that the materiality that was created really expresses the Logos in the world. Rahner himself, in other places, refers to God as the one who creates the humanity of Jesus.

addressee."[25] In other words, if God is going to communicate Godself to that which is not God, God has to create the "not God" that will receive the communication. Thus Rahner calls the human person "Hearer of the Word." Rahner suggests:

> Human nature in general is a possible object of the creative knowledge and power of God, because and insofar as the Logos is by nature the one who is "utterable" (even into that which is not God); because he is the Father's Word, in which the Father can express himself, and, freely, empty himself into the non-divine; because, when this happens, that precisely is born which we call human nature.[26]

Within creation, Rahner notes that "Christ's 'human nature' is not something which happens to be there, among many other things, which might equally well have been hypostatically assumed, but it is precisely that which comes into being when God's Logos 'utters' himself outward."[27] Humanity is created as the potential for incarnation. Rahner explains:

> We see that Christology is at once beginning and end of anthropology, and that for all eternity such an anthropology is really theology. For God "himself" has become "man." The less we merely think of this humanity as something added on to God, and the more we understand it as God's very presence in the world and hence . . . see it in a true spontaneous vitality and freedom before God, the more intelligible does the abiding mystery of our faith become, and also the more does the abiding mystery of our faith become an expression of our own existence.[28]

In the incarnation not only God is revealed to us, but humanity, our own existence and what it means to be a human person, is revealed to us.

---

[25] Rahner, *The Trinity*, 88.

[26] Ibid., 32.

[27] Ibid., 89.

[28] Karl Rahner, "Current Problems in Christology," in *Theological Investigations: God, Christ, Mary, and Grace*, trans. Cornelius Ernst, vol. 1 (Baltimore: Helicon Press, 1961), 185.

Creation and Incarnation

For Rahner, evolution is our worldview, and Christology is congruent with that worldview. Rahner sees a correlation between evolution and transcendence. The human being is understood as enspirited matter. There is no separation of matter and spirit or body and soul. The human person is matter that has become transcendent and self-conscious, and therefore all creation reaches its goal in humanity and Christ. Rahner states:

> For the process by which the cosmos becomes conscious of itself in spiritual subjects must also imply necessarily and above all an intercommunion among these subjects in each of which the whole is present to itself in its own unique way. For otherwise the world's becoming conscious of itself would divide rather than unify.[29]

In other words, in a Bohmian sense of wholeness, Rahner maintains that humanity's consciousness should not create a false division or a hierarchy between humanity and the created world, because there is a wholeness and a unity to creation. In each person's consciousness the cosmos as a whole becomes conscious. Rahner's viewpoint is grounded in scripture from Romans 8:19–21: "For the creation waits with eager longing for the revealing of the children of God; for the creation was subjected to futility, not of its own will but by the will of the one who subjected it, in hope that the creation itself will be set free from its bondage to decay and will obtain the freedom of the glory of the children of God." Christ is the plan and the goal of all creation, not just humanity.

This perspective in which incarnation is the intention of creation from the very beginning is called the Scotistic option, after the theologian Duns Scotus. Building on the tradition of early theologians such as Irenaeus and Maximus, Duns Scotus suggests that Christ be viewed from the perspective of creation rather than as a remedy for sin. Christ is understood as the plan, goal, and culmination to creation. Rahner states:

---

[29] Rahner, *Foundations of Christian Faith*, 193.

> For there is no problem in understanding what is called creation as a partial moment in the process in which God becomes world, and in which God in fact freely expresses himself in his Logos which has become world and matter. We are entirely justified in understanding creation and Incarnation not as two disparate and juxtaposed acts of God "outward" which have their origins in two separate initiatives of God. Rather in the world as it actually is we can understand creation and Incarnation as two moments and two phases of the one process of God's self-giving and self-expression, although it is an intrinsically differentiated process. Such an understanding can appeal to a very old "Christocentric" tradition in the history of Christian theology in which the creative Word of God which establishes the world establishes this world to begin with as the materiality which is to become his own, or to become the environment of his own materiality.[30]

In the one person of Christ, God is united not just to that one human being, but to all creation due to the interconnectedness of reality. Humanity itself is created as that in which God can and does become incarnate. If in the Trinity, God-Logos is the potential within God to "other" Godself, to speak the Word in creation, humanity as Capax Dei is God's mode of being when God "others" Godself. Rahner calls humanity the grammar of God, and hence the image of God. Rather than beginning with human nature as something we are and understand, and then applying that concept of humanity to the incarnation as something that the Logos assumes, Rahner suggests that human nature itself is revealed to us in the incarnation. He asks:

> Is the humanity of the Logos merely something foreign which has been assumed, or is it precisely that which comes into being when the Logos ex-presses himself into the non-divine? Should we start from human nature as from something we already know, as something not more clearly revealed by the incarnation, when we try to explain this incarnation in its real content (with respect to that which the Logos becomes)? Or should human nature *ultimately* be explained through the self-emptying self-utterance of the Logos himself?[31]

[30] Ibid., 197.

[31] Rahner, *The Trinity*, 31n27.

Humanity or human nature is created as part of God's plan to express, reveal, and communicate Godself into creation. We come to understand what it means to be a human person when human personhood is revealed to us in the incarnation of Jesus the Christ.

The Word of God is the plan, the agent, and the goal of creation. Rahner explains:

> We could now define man . . . as that which ensues when God's self-utterance, his Word, is given out lovingly into the void of god-less nothing. Indeed, the Logos made man has been called the abbreviated Word of God. This abbreviation, this code word for God is man, that is, the Son of Man, and men, who exist ultimately because the Son of Man was to exist. . . . If God wills to become non-God, man comes to be.[32]

Humanity is created to be the potential for incarnation. Therefore our anthropology or understanding of what it means to be human can never be separated from our Christology. Rahner states:

> For in this way man becomes precisely someone who participates in the infinite mystery of God, just as a question participates in its answer and just as the question is borne only by the possibility of the answer itself. We know this by the fact that we recognize the incarnate Logos in our history and say: here the question which we are is answered historically and tangibly with God himself.[33]

We exist as a question. In Christ, God answers the question we are by filling that question with the answer that is God's very own self.

Rahner goes on to explain this axiom that Christology is anthropology and theology, or the idea that Christ reveals to us who we are and who God is:

> Because it is the union of the real essence of God and of man in God's personal self-expression in his eternal Logos,

---

[32] Karl Rahner, "On the Theology of the Incarnation," in *Theological Investigations: More Recent Writings*, trans. Kevin Smyth, vol. 4 (Baltimore: Helicon Press, 1966), 116.

[33] Rahner, *Foundations of Christian Faith*, 225.

> for this reason Christology is the beginning and the end of anthropology, and this anthropology in its most radical actualization is for all eternity theology. It is first of all the theology which God himself has spoken by uttering his Word as our flesh into the emptiness of what is not God and is even sinful, and secondly it is the theology which we ourselves do in faith when we do not think that we could find Christ by going around man, and hence find God by going around the human altogether. It could still be said of the creator with the Old Testament that he is in heaven and we are on earth. But we have to say of the God whom we profess in Christ that he is exactly where we are, and only there is he to be found. If nevertheless he remains infinite, this does not mean that he is also still this, but means that the finite itself has received infinite depths. The finite is no longer in opposition to the infinite, but is that which the infinite himself has become, that which he expresses himself as the question which he himself answers. He does this in order to open for the whole of the finite of which he himself has become a part a passage into the infinite—no, I should say in order to make himself the passage and the portal.[34]

Jesus is different from us in that in Jesus we see our potential fulfilled; we see what it means to be fully given over to God. Jesus is that fullness of humanity because he is the fullness of divinity, that is, the incarnate Logos. We are able to be fully given over to God because in grace the Spirit unites us to Christ, and through that union we participate in his fullness of divinity and humanity. God becomes human that we might become divine. What Christ is by nature, we are by adoption.

God and Humanity Do Not Compete

So when the Gospels show Jesus's words and actions as expressing the way he is totally given over to the Father, he is shown to be actualizing who he is, the Logos, as the one utterly dependent on the Father. The Father is the source of the Son. The fact that Jesus is one

[34] Ibid., 226.

with the Logos is precisely the reason he is able to "really do what we cannot do at all: his fundamental attitude and condition (as radical unity of being and consciousness) is radically complete origination from God and dedication to God."[35] Jesus's fundamental attitude is such because his human nature is the symbol, the self-expression of the Logos, who by definition is complete origination from and dedication to God the Father. Jesus lives out that relationship to God the Father in his humanity. Within the limits of his human consciousness, Jesus experiences himself as complete origination from and dedication to God the Father, his Abba. In other words, Jesus experiences himself as the Logos. We too are created to be and live lives of complete origination from and dedication to God. We are created to become human persons in the image of Christ, but we can do so only when we are joined by the Spirit to Christ, who is God's fulfillment of that potential in human nature.

Jesus's human center of activity is never separate from the Logos. The Logos assumes that very center of human activity, and yet, that assumption does not negate the very real limits of humanity that the Logos has assumed, including a human consciousness that would prevent Jesus from knowing in any sort of explicit or cognitive way that he is the eternal Logos. Rather, his identity with the Logos can be seen in the fact that Jesus is entirely given over to the Father. Rahner emphatically maintains:

> The human nature of Jesus is a created, conscious and free reality to which there belongs a created "subjectivity" at least in the sense of a created will, a created *energeia*. This created subjectivity is distinct from the subjectivity of the Logos and faces God at a created distance in freedom, in obedience and in prayer, and it is not omniscient.[36]

Rahner's point is in line with the Third Council of Constantinople, which in 681 asserted that Jesus had both a human will as well as a divine will, against those who said Jesus only had a divine will (monothelitism), and a human center of action as well as a divine center of action against those who said Jesus only had a divine center of action (monoenergism). The council asserted Jesus's full humanity.

---

[35] Karl Rahner, "Jesus Christ," in *Sacramentum Mundi: An Encyclopedia of Theology*, vol. 3 (New York: Herder and Herder, 1969), 200.

[36] Rahner, *Foundations of Christian Faith*, 287.

Thus Jesus is a human person when the word *person* is understood to mean a free, psychological subject in our modern sense of the word, but a divine *person* in the sense of a divine hypostasis (that which bears or stands under the nature, that which makes an individual exist) as the bearer of the human nature. It is precisely this created humanity, this psychological subjectivity, with its finite limits and the distinction from God that those limits of being created entail, that God accepts through the Logos assuming humanity.

The humanity of Jesus and the freedom and actions through which that humanity manifests itself in space and time are the result of the self-expression of God. Consequently, Jesus's human history of freedom and action is always completely dependent on and united to the Logos that it is expressing, which is not to say that Jesus has any explicit consciousness of his action being at the same time the self-expression of the Logos. Rahner often emphasizes the distinction of the humanity of Jesus from the eternal Logos, but in his theology of the symbol he states, "The unity is more original than the distinction, because the symbol is a distinct and yet intrinsic moment of the reality as it manifests itself."[37] It is this unity that allows Jesus to be the self-communication of God to the world. The humanity of Jesus is always united to the person of the Logos. If it were completely independent of the Logos, Jesus's life and death could not be revelatory of God. In such a case, Jesus would not make God present in the world, but would be one more prophet pointing to God, a word about God able to be surpassed by some new or higher revelation.

Rahner maintains that utter dependence on God and complete autonomy are not contradictory at all, but rather exist in direct proportion to one another. For Rahner, this axiom relates to all creatures and to Jesus Christ specifically. Rahner understands the freedom of Jesus's human nature to exist precisely *because* it subsists in the person of the divine Logos. In other words, Jesus's human freedom makes him truly free and autonomous in his humanity because that freedom is completely dependent on the divine Logos. The more one is dependent upon God, the more perfectly free one is. He states that "only a *divine* Person can possess as its own a freedom really distinct from itself in such a way that this freedom does not cease to be truly free even with regard to the divine Person possessing it, while it continues to

---

[37] Karl Rahner, "The Theology of the Symbol," in *Theological Investigations,* 4:221–52.

qualify this very Person as its ontological subject."[38] He grounds this understanding of the relationship between the human nature and the divine person in his theological anthropology. Rahner asserts:

> There also applies here . . . the axiom for understanding every relationship between God and creature, namely, that closeness and distance, or being at God's disposal and being autonomous, do not vary for creatures in inverse, but rather in direct proportion. Christ is therefore man in the most radical way, and his humanity is the most autonomous and the most free not in spite of, but because it has been assumed, because it has been created as God's self-expression.[39]

For Rahner, the ability to have any sort of autonomy is grounded in one's dependence on God.

Given that "definition" of autonomy, Rahner can say that Jesus's human nature is the most autonomous, but only insofar as that nature subsists in the person of the Logos. Rahner argues that "we must conceive of the relation between the Logos-Person and his human nature in just this sense, that here *both* independence *and* radical proximity reach a unique and qualitatively incommensurable perfection, which nevertheless remains once and for all the perfection of a relation between Creator and creature."[40] Any freedom and autonomy that Jesus has as human is grounded in the Logos and is appropriated by the Logos, thus it is the freedom and autonomy of the Logos as well—which is to say, it is the *human* freedom and autonomy of the Logos. This absolute freedom grounded in absolute dependence on God is the perfection of what it means to be a human person, a perfection that is only achieved in the hypostatic union and which the rest of humanity can only participate in through Jesus Christ. For Rahner, "the more radically any given individual is related to God existentially, and so too in his concrete mode of

[38] Rahner, "Current Problems in Christology," 162. Rahner footnotes the fact that the independence of the Logos is understood as the freedom of the human nature and the radical proximity is the substantial appropriation by the Logos of this human nature *and* its freedom.

[39] Rahner, *Foundations of Christian Faith*, 226; see also Rahner, "On the Theology of the Incarnation," 117.

[40] Rahner, "Current Problems in Christology," 162–63..

existence as a creature, the more such a creature achieves the state of self-realization; again the more radically any given individual is able to experience his own creaturely reality, the more united he must be with God."[41] The more human one becomes, the more united with God one is, because God and humanity do not compete. Jesus is the perfection of humanity and can only be so because he is the incarnate Logos. The fact that the human nature of Jesus subsists in the divine hypostasis of the Logos does not separate him from humanity; it makes him the universal fulfillment of the potential that is found in every human, that is to say, it is what makes him *fully* human. Thus we understand what it means to be a human person connected to the wholeness that is God as Source of Love in and through the person of Jesus Christ who is the perfect expression of a human person.

Jesus is the perfection of this direct proportion between dependence on God and the autonomy to be what God has created one to be because of *God's* action in constituting him as such. It is not something that Jesus achieves or something that another human being can achieve, except in relative terms. Jesus is our mediator because everything Jesus does in his human life is the revelation of God through the incarnate Logos, and yet everything that Jesus does, he does through the exercise of his human freedom. Rahner makes this point by emphasizing that "this human history, by the very fact of being God's own pure and radical revelation, is the most living of all, the most free before God from the world towards God, and thus mediatorial, because it is the history of God himself *and* because it is supremely creaturely and free."[42]

---

[41] Karl Rahner, "The Position of Christology in the Church between Exegesis and Dogmatics," in *Theological Investigations: Confrontations I*, trans. David Bourke, vol. 11 (New York: Seabury, 1974), 199.

[42] Rahner, "Current Problems in Christology," 163. Rahner is able to maintain this both/and position because of the mutual, subsistent relationship between the person of the Logos and the human nature of Jesus, that is, through the enhypostasia. The person of the Logos subsists in Jesus's human history, thus mediating God to the world and the world to God through the human nature that is distinct from the eternal Logos but always in unity with the Logos. For further discussion of this dual understanding of *subsistence*, which includes not only the human nature subsisting in the hypostasis of the Logos, but also the hypostasis of the Logos subsisting in the human nature, see David Coffey, "The Theandric Nature of Christ," *Theological Studies* 60, no. 3 (1999): 417–18.

Jesus is not a prophet revealing something about God, but rather the incarnate Logos, the self-expression of God to creation, thus truly revealing Godself. Therefore, any free and independent action of Jesus as human, such as prayer, obedience, death, and so forth, is the action of the Logos, whose reality is being expressed in that creaturely distinction. It is the action of the Logos, but only insofar as it is the action of the Logos *as* human, that is, the way the Logos acts when the Logos has assumed human nature and accepted all of the limitations of that created humanity. The unity of the human nature and the divine nature of Jesus in the divine hypostasis does not make Jesus less human; rather, it is precisely what makes Jesus *fully* human, a human being or a human person (that is, a psychological subject) in the deepest sense of what it means to be human. We, in turn, understand what it means to be a human person in and through our union with Jesus Christ.

The Holy Spirit as the Love of God Poured into Our Hearts

Whereas the hypostatic union, which is to say the oneness of the hypostasis in Christ, or more simply, the fact that there is only one individual who is both human and divine, effects the union between humanity and divinity in the person of Christ, grace effects our union with God. The Holy Spirit as the love of God that has been poured into our hearts (Rom 5:5) joins us to that union of God and humanity that takes place in the person of Jesus Christ. Rahner notes:

> Consequently, anyone who, though still far from any revelation explicitly formulated in words, accepts his existence in patient silence (or, better, in faith, hope and love), accepts it as the mystery which lies hidden in the mystery of eternal love and which bears life in the womb of death, is saying "yes" to Christ even if he does not know it. For anyone who lets go and jumps falls into the depths which are there, and not only to the extent that he himself has fathomed them. Anyone who accepts his humanity fully, and all the more so of course the humanity of others, has accepted the Son of Man because in him God has

> accepted man. And if it says in scripture that whoever loves his neighbor has fulfilled the law, then this is the ultimate truth because God has become this neighbor, and hence He who is at once nearest to us and farthest from us is always accepted and loved in every neighbor.[43]

Yet on our own we do not have the ability to achieve that God-filled humanity that is revealed in the incarnation. We need the gift of the Holy Spirit, God's love poured into our hearts. The Spirit is the power and action of God in the world and in our lives acting in and through us, acting in and through history. The Spirit in us unites us to Christ, joins our yes to his, forming us into the body of Christ. In the Spirit we become the ongoing sacramental presence of God in the world. As the body of Christ we are called to be the mediation of God's unconditional love and forgiveness in the world. In the Spirit the wholeness of God as Love that has been enfolded in us is unfolded in the world, making us realize our interconnectedness to one another and forming us into community.

God the Father utters the Word into history, thus revealing and communicating Godself to us in the incarnation, but God also reveals and offers Godself to us through the Holy Spirit in the gift of grace. Rahner argues that the Trinity is not a doctrine we are taught but rather a reality we experience. Church teaching about the Trinity helps make manifest the reality that is always already present at the core of our being. Rahner suggests that "we can really grasp the content of the Trinity only by going back to the history of salvation and of grace, to our experience of Jesus and of the Spirit of God, who operates in us, because in them we really already possess the Trinity itself as such."[44] Rahner explains that the Holy Spirit, as the self-communication of God, "is God as given in love and powerful in us in love."[45] The Holy Spirit is God the Father communicating Godself to us "as love and forgiveness" in a manner that is "distinct from the Father who gives and from the Son who mediates."[46]

---

[43] Rahner, *Foundations of Christian Faith*, 228.
[44] Rahner, *The Trinity*, 40.
[45] Ibid., 66.
[46] Ibid., 66–67.

The Spirit as Offer and Acceptance of Love

In the Spirit, God gives Godself to us as offer. That offer is the self-gift or self-communication of God as Love that has been revealed to us in the person of Jesus Christ. That offer exists in each one of us at the core of our being through the indwelling of the Holy Spirit. God doesn't give us something other than God. God gives God's own self to us. In doing so, "God in his own most proper reality makes himself the innermost constitutive element of man."[47] Rahner calls God's offer of self that is the gift of the Holy Spirit the "supernatural existential." The offer is supernatural, because it is God giving Godself to us.[48] Rahner explains that this offer of self is always a free gift that is never owed to us: "God's self-communication is a further miracle of his free love which is the most self-evident thing of all, and at the same time cannot be logically deduced from anything else."[49] It is existential because it is offered and exists within each and every person as the core of their being. Even in the face of its rejection, that grace that is the Spirit continues to exist in the person as offer, hence redemption is always a possibility.

Rahner notes that the offer is made to all people. It belongs intrinsically to each and every human being as part of who we are, not as something extrinsic and added on to who we are, but as the innermost core of our being. Rahner states, "In the only order that is real, the emptiness of the transcendental creature exists because the fullness of God creates this emptiness in order to communicate himself to it."[50] The universality of this offer to every single person makes it no less gratuitous. It is not owed to us just because it is offered to all of us. It is still a free gift given to all. Furthermore, the offer does not cease to be supernatural—that is, of God—by virtue of the fact that it is made to everyone. The offer of Godself as Love to all humankind is a manifestation of God's universal salvific will, and it is permanent. The offer continues to exist as offer, even when rejected.

---

47 Rahner, *Foundations of Christian Faith*, 116.

48 Note that "supernatural" here means beyond our nature. Super as a prefix means above or beyond, in the way a superscript is a number above the text. "Supernatural" means "above" the natural, meaning it is God, not human.

49 Rahner, *Foundations of Christian Faith*, 123.

50 Ibid.

We have the ability to reject, through our freedom, that gift of the Spirit that is God's self-communication existing in us as an offer. But if we do not reject that offer, the offer itself is efficacious, enabling us to accept God's offer of love that is Godself.[51] However, that enabled acceptance can never take place in one single act. It takes place over the course of our lifetime and is always an acceptance that is commingled with all of the ways in which we reject God's offer of love. Our yes is always mixed with no. That is why the Holy Spirit unites our finite and partial yes to the infinite and absolute yes of Jesus Christ on the cross. Rahner concludes:

> A person who opens himself to his transcendental experience of the holy mystery at all has the experience that this mystery is not only an infinitely distant horizon, a remote judgment which judges from a distance his consciousness and his world of persons and things, it is not only something mysterious which frightens him away and back into the confines of his everyday world. He experiences rather that this holy mystery is also a hidden closeness, a forgiving intimacy, his real home, that it is a love which shares itself, something familiar which he can approach and turn to from the estrangement of his own perilous and empty life. It is the person who in the forlornness of his guilt turns in trust to the mystery of his existence which is quietly present, and surrenders himself as one who in his guilt no longer wants to understand himself in a self-centered and self-sufficient way, it is this person who experiences himself as one who does not forgive himself, but who is forgiven, and he experiences this forgiveness which he receives as the hidden, forgiving and liberating love of God himself, who forgives in that he gives himself, because only in this way can there really be forgiveness once and for all.[52]

In this experience of the Holy Spirit as grace, God's self-gift of love, we experience ourselves as forgiven. Each and every day of our lives we could be more, we could love more. Our yes is finite and partial.

---

[51] Heidi Russell, "Efficacious and Sufficient Grace: God's One Offer or Self-Communication as Accepted or Rejected," *Philosophy and Theology* 22, no. 1–2 (2010): 353–72.

[52] Rahner, *Foundations of Christian Faith*, 131.

We give, so long as it is not too hard and does not demand too much of us. We experience the grace and mercy of God in the glimpses we have of all the ways we fall short and the love that both accepts us as we are and calls us to be more.

Rahner follows a tradition of Christian theology in which God the Source of All Love expresses Godself in the world through the incarnate Word of Love and enacts that Love in the world through the Holy Spirit of Love. Incarnation and grace reveal the Trinity to us. For Rahner, these revelations do not reveal something about God to us; rather, they reveal Godself, because the communication of God is a self-communication, a gift of self. I suggest they also reveal something about us. The incarnation reveals what it means to be a human person, fully autonomous and conscious. The Spirit reveals what it means to be community, enabled through grace to live lives of self-actualization and love through our relationships with one another. The Trinity reveals to us catholicity, the wholeness of love. The Love that has been enfolded into each one of us, enabling us to become sons (and daughters) in the Son, or, one might say, persons in the person of Christ, is unfolded into the world in and through the network of interrelatedness that makes us the body of Christ, the ongoing revelation of God as Love in the world.

Chapter 6

From a Social Analogy to the Analogy of Love

Advocates of a social Trinitarianism or a social analogy of the Trinity[1] have raised certain objections to what is often referred to as Latin Trinitarianism or monotheistic Trinitarianism.[2] Three objections raised are the ideas that Latin Trinitarianism focuses on interiority (focusing on our inner selves) to the detriment of intersubjectivity (our inherent relationality), individuality to the detriment of community, and the immanent Trinity (God in Godself) to the detriment of the economic Trinity (God acting in creation and salvation). Social trinitarians claim to address these concerns through the trinitarian image of three Persons in mutual and equal communion with one another.

---

[1] Note that some social trinitarians can be outright tritheists (for example, Richard Swinburne), whereas those who propose a social analogy of the Trinity are doing so analogously and thus, while there is a danger of tritheism in the analogy, would not claim to be tritheists.

[2] Both terms are problematic. *Latin* refers to the legacy of Augustine. Scholars such as Michel Barnes ("Rereading Augustine's Theology of the Trinity") and Sarah Coakley ("'Persons' in the 'Social' Doctrine of the Trinity: Current Analytic Discussion and 'Cappadocian' Theology") would point out that the distinction between Augustine and the Cappadocians is not as clear cut as some would suggest. Both essays are in Stephen Davis, Daniel Kendall, and Gerald O'Collins, eds., *The Trinity: An Interdisciplinary Symposium on the Trinity* (Oxford: Oxford University Press, 1999). *Monotheistic* implies that the other theories are not *monotheistic,* and most who purport a social analogy of the Trinity do claim to be monotheistic.

The challenges that the social trinitarians offer to Latin Trinitarianism are valid. Their solution is to reconceive the concept of the human person in light of what *Person* means in the Trinity. The question for those who do not accept social Trinitarianism then becomes whether or not there is a way of talking about Trinity that can address these concerns without being subject to the possible misconception of tritheism and without understanding God as three beings, subjects, or consciousnesses in relationship with one another. The word *person* is at the heart of this issue. The argument of the social trinitarians is that rather than letting the modern history of the word, in which it means an individual with freedom and consciousness, change our understanding of the Trinity, an effort should be made to let the Trinity change our meaning of the word *person.* They suggest that doing so could thereby transform what has been understood as a rational and conscious individual into an understanding of person that focuses on mutuality, intersubjectivity, and that which only comes to be in relationality—allowing what LaCugna calls a metaphysics of relation to replace a metaphysics of substance.[3] While the efforts to reconceptualize the meaning of *person* are both laudable and necessary, mutuality, intersubjectivity, and relationality are generally notions that are added on to the understanding of the person as individual rather than replacing person as individual. In other words, when we think of intersubjectivity, we think of two individual subjects. When we think of mutuality, we think of two individuals in a relationship of equality and reciprocity. When we think of relationality, we think of two individual beings relating to each other in an experience of coming to know and understand each one in relationship to the other. The problem with this approach is that the modern, popular understanding of person as individual subject overrides the new definition in popular images of God as Trinity, leading to a practical misconception among a popular audience, which conceives of the Trinity as three individual beings relating to one another.

---

[3] Catherine Mowry LaCugna, *God for Us: The Trinity and Christian Life* (San Francisco: HarperSanFrancisco, 1991), 243. See also idem, "The Relational God: Aquinas and Beyond," *Theological Studies* 46 (1995): 647–63; and idem, "Philosophers and Theologians on the Trinity," *Modern Theology* 2, no. 3 (1986): 169–81.

The Social Analogy of the Trinity in Jürgen Moltmann and Leonardo Boff

None of the social theorists of the Trinity presents his or her model as definitive. All recognize with humility the limits of human words and concepts and see their models as one analogy among many. Likewise, the alternative model offered in this book is not intended to be exclusive, but rather in conversation with other analogies, in order to help correct the potential excesses in any one analogy. For all the helpful pastoral implications of the social theory of the Trinity, there is a danger of reading this metaphor in a literal way, invoking an image of three people sitting around a table in the imaginations of the faithful. That image can and must be countered with a new image that moves away from depicting God as three individual beings.

Jürgen Moltmann's major issue with traditional trinitarian theology is the correspondence between what he calls metaphysical monotheism and political monarchy resulting in imperialism.[4] In other words, Moltmann's concern is that our focus on the Godhead as a subject to the exclusion of the trinitarian persons has historically resulted in a legitimation of political monarchies in which the king was viewed as a corollary to God. A further result of this correlation of power is patriarchy. Such a correspondence between the political ruler and the cosmic ruler is a direct result of imaging God as a being, in the sense of an entity. As a corrective to this monotheism, "the essence of Moltmann's position is that when it comes to divine action we have three subjects, or *loci*, of activity, not one. We have three persons, not one."[5] Moltmann's Trinity of three subjects thus has power distributed among equals rather than located in the hands of one individual.

The problem with this image of three subjects sharing power is that it raises the issue of tritheism or a belief in three gods. Veli-Matti Kärkkäinen notes: "One frequent question to Moltmann and other social Trinitarians is whether they have ended up affirming tritheism

---

[4] Jürgen Moltmann, *Sun of Righteousness, Arise! God's Future for Humanity and the Earth*, trans. Margaret Kohl (Minneapolis: Fortress Press, 2010), 87–88.

[5] Ted Peters, *God as Trinity: Relationality and Temporality in Divine Life* (Louisville, KY: Westminster/John Knox Press, 1993), 104. For Peters's critique of Moltmann in this regard, see 109–10.

in their fear of 'monotheism.' Scholars from a wide variety of orientations have expressed strong concerns about tritheism; some even leveled the charge of tritheism."[6]

Moltmann uses the concept of perichoresis, the idea that the three encompass one another and act as one together, to explain the unity of the three Persons, and with this concept he argues that "it becomes possible to conceive of a community without uniformity and a personhood without individualism."[7] Moltmann also focuses on the complete equality of the Persons, highlighting "the triadic intersubjectivity" of perichoresis. Again the problem is that when one speaks of intersubjectivity of the Trinity, the implication is a relationship among three subjects. Moltmann seems to avoid the image of God as one absolute subject by replacing this notion with a God who is three subjects in communion and perichoresis with one another. Moltmann maintains that he is not using Boethius's definition of person,

> because in the perichoresis the trinitarian persons cannot be individual substances or individuals resting in themselves and existing from themselves. They are rather to be understood as ex-static hypostases. We need a perichoretic concept of *person*. . . . By virtue of their selfless love, the trinitarian persons come to themselves in one another.[8]

Moltmann wants to use the Trinity to redefine our concept of person as coming to be in and for another. In actual practice, however, the danger is that the word as it is defined by society will shape people's understanding of God rather than vice versa.

Moltmann also notes that the unity of the Trinity is not exclusive or closed, but is open and inviting,[9] and that

> the inviting, integrating and uniting community of the Triune God . . . is "open," not out of deficiency or incompleteness, but

---

[6] Veli-Matti Kärkkäinen, *The Trinity: Global Perspectives* (Louisville, KY: Westminster John Knox Press, 2007), 115; cf. 122n, 123n.

[7] Moltmann, *Sun of Righteousness, Arise!*, 153.

[8] Ibid., 156. Cf. Karen Kilby, "Perichoresis and Projection: Problems with Social Doctrines of the Trinity," *New Blackfriars* 81 (2001): 441–42. See also Randall Otto, "The Use and Abuse of Perichoresis in Recent Theology," *Scottish Journal of Theology* 54 (2001): 366–84.

[9] Moltmann, *Sun of Righteousness, Arise!*, 156.

> in the overflow of love, which gives created beings the living space for their livingness and scope for their development.[10]

The church as community should be modeled on the Trinity, so that the church is also open and inviting, a living space of overflowing love. For Moltmann, the triunity of God functions to form the community of church fellowship that

> does not just "correspond" to the trinitarian unity of God; but it also "exists" in the triunity of God which is open to the world; for through the efficacy of the Father, the Son and the Spirit it is taken into the inner mystery of God. The open space of the perichoretic sociality of the triune God is the church's divine living space.[11]

The practical implications of this divine life can be seen in the Acts of the Apostles, where

> this so-called early Christian communism was not a social programme; it was the expression of the new trinitarian experience of sociality. These Christians put their community above the individual and above their private possessions. . . . This community ends the competitive struggle which turns people into lonely individuals, and the social frigidity of a heartless world disappears.[12]

For Moltmann, the church is only able to be this open, life-giving community because it exists within the Triune God.

As with Moltmann, Leonardo Boff wants to use the Trinity to redefine our understanding of communion or community. He primarily argues that doing so has vast implications for the way we live as society and as church. Boff defines the Trinity as "the Father, the Son and the Holy Spirit in eternal correlation, interpenetration and love, to the extent that they form one God."[13] Boff argues against the tradi-

---

[10] Ibid., 157.

[11] Ibid., 162.

[12] Ibid. Moltmann cites 1 Corinthians 12:4–6 and Acts 4:32–37 as examples of this trinitarian experience of community.

[13] Leonardo Boff, *Trinity and Society*, trans. Paul Burns (Maryknoll, NY: Orbis Books, 1988), 9.

tional understandings of Trinity that ground unity of the three Persons in either the monarchy of the Father or the divine nature/substance.[14] For Boff, trinitarian theology should start

> from the Trinity of Persons—Father, Son, and Holy Spirit. But the Three live in eternal perichoresis, being one in the others, through the others, with the others and for the others. The unity of the Trinity means the union of the three Persons by virtue of their perichoresis and eternal communion. Since this union is eternal and infinite, we can speak of one God.[15]

Boff himself warns of the "risk of tritheism," but he claims that this understanding of Trinity

> avoids it through perichoresis and through general communion existing from the beginning between the Three Persons. We are not to think that originally the Three existed on their own, separate from the others, coming only later into communion and perichoretic relationship. . . . No, the Persons are intrinsically and from all eternity bound up with each other.[16]

The notion that the three are eternally in relationship with one another, however, does not prevent conceptualizing the three as three beings in relationship with one another. Boff tries to avoid the charge of tritheism through the notion that in God there is one consciousness, but three conscious subjects.[17] As Kärkkäinen notes, even while defending Boff against charges of tritheism, the question must be asked what it means to have a conscious subject without a distinct consciousness.[18]

Like Moltmann, Boff attempts to use the Trinity to redefine the concept of person while also noting the difficulties with this word when used in trinitarian theology.[19] For Boff, Persons, as understood

---

[14] Ibid., 4.
[15] Ibid., 234–35.
[16] Ibid., 5–6.
[17] Ibid., 115.
[18] Kärkkäinen, *The Trinity*, 290.
[19] Boff, *Trinity and Society*, 7–8.

in the Trinity, "are intrinsically open to others, exist with others and are one for one another."[20] He explains:

> In the light of the Trinity, being a person in the image and likeness of the divine Persons means acting as a permanently active web of relationships: relating backward and upward to one's origin in the unfathomable mystery of the Father, relating outward to one's fellow human beings by revealing oneself to them and welcoming the revelation of them in the mystery of the Son, relating inward to the depths of one's own personality in the mystery of the Trinity.[21]

The concept of person given by Boff is a needed reconceptualization, but it does not require an understanding of the Trinity in which "the persons are three infinite subjects of a single communion, or three lovers in the same love."[22]

Boff concurs with the idea of using the economic Trinity as revealed in scripture to explain the relationship of the Three in the Trinity. The problem in Boff's approach arises in using the economic Trinity in such a way that it does not take into account the humanity of Jesus. Boff, in talking about the relationship between the Father and the Son, notes: "Jesus' relationship with his Father reveals a certain distance and distinction, along with a deep intimacy. Distinction is revealed in the fact that Jesus prays and prostrates himself in God's presence. Intimacy is evinced in his name for God: Papa."[23] Such distance, however, is due to the humanity of Jesus, the kenosis of accepting the created reality of human nature and necessarily by fact of that creaturehood experiencing existence as an individual related to God the Father through the power of the Holy Spirit. That created humanity, in hypostatic union with the Word of God, then becomes the self-expression, the self-revelation of God as Love in the world.

---

[20] Ibid., 5.

[21] Ibid., 149.

[22] Leonardo Boff, "Trinity," in *Mysterium Liberationis: Fundamental Concepts of Liberation Theology*, ed. Ignacio Ellacuría and Jon Sobrino (Maryknoll, NY: Orbis Books, 1993), 398.

[23] Ibid., 393.

The key point for Boff in this model of Trinity is the implication for liberation. Boff maintains, "The oppressed struggle for participation at all levels of life, for a just and egalitarian sharing while respecting the differences between persons and groups."[24] He goes on to explain:

> The trinitarian communion between the divine Three, the union between them in love and vital interpenetration, can serve as a source of inspiration, as a utopian goal that generates models of successively diminishing differences. . . . The community of Father, Son and Holy Spirit becomes the prototype of the human community dreamed of by those who wish to improve society and build it in such a way as to make it into the image and likeness of the Trinity.[25]

The implications of this vision of communion, for Boff, encompass society, the church, and the poor. Boff argues:

> *Society* offends the Trinity by organizing itself on a basis of inequality and honours it the more it favours sharing and communion for all, thereby bringing about justice and equality for all. The *church* is more the sacrament of trinitarian communion the more it reduces inequalities between Christians and between the various ministries in it, and the more it understands and practices unity as co-existence in diversity. The *poor* reject their impoverishment as sin against trinitarian communion and see the inter-relatedness of the divine "Differents" as the model for a human society based on mutual collaboration—all on an equal footing—and based on individual differences; that society's structures would be humane, open, just, and egalitarian.[26]

For Boff, both a concept of the monarchy of the Father and an a-trinitarian monotheism has led to political dominance in earthly monarchies and dictatorships and a concentration of ecclesial power in the papacy.[27] Both of these issues of dominant rulers come from an

---

[24] Boff, *Trinity and Society*, 6.
[25] Ibid., 6–7.
[26] Ibid., 236–37.
[27] Ibid., 152–53.

imaging of the ruler that mirrors an imaging of God, and that image of God is God as Being, or more particularly, God as *a being*.

Boff uses the social Trinity to criticize both capitalism and socialism for their lack of acceptance of difference and diversity.[28] For Boff, the antidote to this domination and collectivization is the Trinity, "precisely in its being a communion of three different beings; in it, mutual acceptance of differences is the vehicle for the plural unity of the three divine Persons."[29]

Boff also criticizes capitalism for valuing individual differences "to the detriment of communion"[30] in the emphasis on private property and exclusive ownership. Boff warns that

> a society that takes its inspiration from trinitarian communion cannot tolerate class differences, dominations based on power (economic, sexual, or ideological) that subjects those who are different to those who exercise that power and marginalizes the former from the latter.[31]

Boff notes, "The catholicity of the church resides in the respect and welcome it affords to the gifts and specialties the Spirit gives to each local church. All local churches are united through the risen Christ, in the Spirit," but he bases this communion in the concept that "the three Uniques are one God in communion."[32]

An Alternative Model to Moltmann and Boff

A new approach to address the concerns of the social theorists is to reconceive the Trinity in terms of love rather than person, and then to reconceive what it means to be a person in light of the incarnation of Love in the human person, the divinized humanity, of Jesus Christ. Likewise, society/communion can be reconceived in light of the Spirit acting in and through the human community, creating the church as the body of Christ, the ongoing revelation of God as Love

---

[28] Ibid., 149–51.
[29] Ibid., 150.
[30] Boff, "Trinity," 400.
[31] Boff, *Trinity and Society*, 151.
[32] Ibid., 153.

and wholeness in the world. The economic Trinity as God for us does not just reveal God to us. It also reveals humanity to us, because the economic Trinity is God in relationship to humanity. Therefore, in that relationship between God and humanity we can reconceive what it means to be person in Christ and what it means to be community in the Spirit-filled Christian and catholic community that unfolds the wholeness of God's love in the world. The economic Trinity also reveals God to us in such a way that we can say something about the immanent Trinity or who God is in Godself, because the God that is communicated to us in incarnation and grace is who God really is in Godself. The God that is communicated to us is a God who is Love, Expressed and Enacted, thus God who is Unoriginate Source of Love, Word of Love, and Spirit of Love.

In the person and revelation of Jesus Christ we see an example of incarnate Love who is a person living in and for others, creating space for others, sharing self and power with others, while building a community that is inviting, integrating, and uniting, grounded in an overflow of love. Thus the human person of Jesus Christ reveals what it means to be a person in a way that accomplishes all of what Moltmann wants to attribute to the Three of the Trinity. It is not the immanent Trinity that reveals person to us, it is Love incarnate.

Leonardo Boff offers a needed corrective to how we understand the human person, but rather than grounding that example of being a human person in the Persons of the Trinity, we find that person who is intrinsically open to others, exists with others, and is one for one another in the incarnate person of Jesus Christ.[33] In that incarnational image that reveals to us what it means to be a human person, human persons can understand themselves as relating backward and upward to their origin in love as Jesus does to his Abba. They also relate outward to all humanity through a revelation of self and an openness to the revelation of the other that reveals each to be a manifestation of the presence of Love to which they are united. Finally, they relate inward to the action of Love within them and working through them unfolding their wholeness in the world.

The community of Acts is indeed a community that is an expression of the Trinity, but not because it is modeled on the relations of the Persons in the Trinity. The early Christian community revealed in Acts expresses the Trinity because it unfolds God as Love by being

[33] Ibid., 5.

the means or sacrament of Love in the world through the action of the Holy Spirit. God acts in and through the community as the indwelling Spirit, thus forming it into the body of Christ. God as Love is now revealed and enacted through the community, which by the power of the indwelling Spirit becomes the manifestation of God's love in the world. Moltmann himself notes, love presupposes difference and creates space for the other as other without totalizing the other.[34] A community that is the sacrament of God as Love is not a community of individuals in competition with one another, but rather a community of persons modeled on the image of person found in Jesus Christ, sharing self, power, and possessions with one another as was witnessed in the scriptural accounts of the early Christian communities (Acts 2:42–47; 4:32–35).

Such excesses in society as are enumerated by Leonardo Boff can also be critiqued in light of understanding our existence as individuals to be forged out of love and thus created in a manner that is always, already interconnected as a whole. Such excesses and rampant inequality are counter to catholicity or the wholeness of love. The witness of Jesus, the incarnate Word revealing God as Love in the world, and his attitude toward ownership as well as the witness of the early community in Acts empowered by the Spirit and its common ownership of goods are the model for us to understand what it means to be an individual in community rather than understanding the Persons of the Trinity as individuals in community.

One need not image God as three Persons relating to one another to make such a critique of society. Rather, if one understands God in terms of love rather than being and sees the Holy Spirit as the power of that love, then a society that is grounded in belief in such a God also cannot tolerate domination based on power, because power has been redefined as the power of love, the power which makes all equal, a power that has been revealed and exemplified in Jesus Christ.

Boff's concerns can be addressed without resorting to a model of the Trinity that lends itself to a tritheistic conceptualization. The witness of the New Testament is not the interrelationship of the trinitarian

---

[34] Moltmann, *Son of Righteousness, Arise!,* 151. Jean-Luc Marion notes that "loving requires an exteriority that is not provisional but effective, an exteriority that remains for long enough that one may cross it seriously. Loving requires distance and the crossing of distance." *The Erotic Phenomenon*, trans. Stephen E. Lewis (Chicago: University of Chicago Press, 2007), 46.

Three forming communion and society with one another, but rather the power of God as Love enacted in community and society as witnessed by the early Christian community in the Acts of the Apostles, where all things were held in common and were divided among all according to each one's need (Acts 2:44–45).

The diversity of the local churches highlighted by Boff can also be understood through the presence of the Spirit enacting God as Love. In scripture the Spirit manifests itself as the power and action of God as Love in the unity of the diverse Christian communities. The Pauline, pastoral, and Johannine letters witness an incredible diversity of community, practice, and ministries, but a union of belief, breaking bread, and being the body of Christ, the sacrament of God as love in the world. As Richard Gaillardetz notes, "The Holy Spirit does not erase difference but renders difference non-divisive."[35] Likewise leadership in the church today need not be built on a monarchical model of power over, but rather can be (and is) understood as servant leadership that is revealed in the person of Jesus Christ and his foot washing relationship to the community he gathers. Jesus, the incarnate Word manifesting God as Love, does not hoard power, but rather shares his power with his followers, sending them out two by two to do the very things that he has done, to manifest God's love in the world, healing the sick and proclaiming the reign of God (Lk 10:1ff.). The resurrected Christ sends the Spirit upon the community, the very Spirit of God as Love that was acting in him now present and acting in them, forming them into the body of Christ, enabling them to do what Christ had done, to be Christ in the world and manifest God's love to all.

God acts in and through this community by the power of the Holy Spirit dwelling within and among these persons in Christ. Thus the immanent Trinity that is God in Godself as Source, Word, Spirit of Love is revealed in the economic Trinity through the person of Jesus Christ and the indwelling grace of the Holy Spirit. God for us reveals not simply God in Godself, but God in relationship to us—God in unity with humanity in the incarnation revealing what it means to be a human person and God in unity with humanity in grace revealing what it means to be community.

---

[35] Richard Gaillardetz, *Ecclesiology for a Global Church: A People Called and Sent* (Maryknoll, NY: Orbis Books, 2008), 38.

The Trinitarian Theology of Catherine Mowry LaCugna

Much of Catherine LaCugna's trinitarian theology resonates with the image of Trinity proposed in this work.[36] Her emphasis on God as love, her focus on the economic Trinity, and especially her concept of God as ineffable mystery evoking praise are congruent with the idea of God as Unoriginate Source of Love revealed in Word and enacted in Spirit. However, she is often characterized with the social trinitarians because she falls back on images and terms of three Persons in a communion of love, using them (and pronouns such as *them*) as a model for what being relational means among human persons. When LaCugna makes statements such as "God exists as diverse persons united in a communion of freedom, love, and knowledge,"[37] it can mislead readers into thinking of the Trinity as three individuals in a manner similar to Boff.

Drawing on the Cappadocians and Orthodox theologian John Zizioulas, LaCugna primarily argues for the use of the category of person in order to emphasize that God is personal.[38] God must be understood first and foremost as relational. LaCugna explains that, "the *esse* [being] of God is to-be-related, and the activity proper to such a being is relating. Thus to be God is to-be-relationally. . . . God is personal *because* God is relational, and not vice versa."[39] While LaCugna does follow the social trinitarians in using the imagery of three persons in community, she is more concerned with the understanding of God as *personal* rather than as Person. She maintains:

> It does not so much matter whether we say God is one person in three modalities, or one nature in three persons, since these two assertions can be understood in approximately the same way. What matters is that we hold on to the assertion that God is *personal*, and that therefore the proper subject matter of the

---

[36] For an accessible and abbreviated summary of LaCugna's position, see Catherine Mowry LaCugna, "The Practical Trinity," *Christian Century* 109, no. 22 (2000): 15–22.

[37] LaCugna, *God for Us*, 243.

[38] Ibid., 244–45.

[39] LaCugna, "The Relational God," 654.

> doctrine of the Trinity is the encounter between divine and human persons in the economy of redemption.[40]

LaCugna follows Zizioulas and the Eastern tradition in grounding personhood in the monarchy of the Father, hence her ability to be fluid in her approach to whether God is spoken of as one Person or three Persons. She argues that *person* must be redefined in relational terms rather than understanding person as "an individual who is self-possessed in self-knowledge and self-love."[41] LaCugna explains that "a person is defined by relation of origin ('from-another')" and so "the divine persons are never thought of as separate from each other, as discrete individuals."[42] In other words, she tries to sidestep the issue that speaking of three Persons in the Trinity suggests three individuals by redefining *person* as "from another." The Son is "from another" in being begotten by the Father. The Spirit is "from another" by proceeding from the Father (and the Son in the Western tradition).

Given her emphasis on the economic Trinity or God for us, LaCugna maintains that "the divine essence is indeed revealed, given, bestowed in Christ, but what is given is not an impersonal nature, an 'in-itself,' but the highest, most perfect realization of personhood and communion: being-for-another and from-another, or love itself."[43] LaCugna "suggests not only that we abandon the misleading terms, economic and immanent Trinity, but that we also clarify the meaning of *oikonomia* and *theologia*" as more simply the "plan of God" and the "mystery of God."[44] Her point is that we never know who God is in Godself, the immanent Trinity, beyond what God reveals of Godself in the world. God is ultimately mystery. However, God has a plan of salvation and has revealed Godself in the Son and Spirit. Thus LaCugna notes that it is the person of Jesus Christ who "discloses what it means to be fully personal, divine as well as human," and the Holy Spirit that "gathers us together into the body of Christ, transforming us so that 'we become by grace what God is by nature,' namely, persons in full communion with God and with every

---

40 LaCugna, *God for Us*, 305.

41 Ibid., 14.

42 Ibid., 246.

43 Ibid.

44 Ibid., 223.

creature."[45] LaCugna wants to redefine what we mean by person using the economic Trinity as our model.[46]

LaCugna broadens the concept of communion and wants to focus primarily on the communion between God and the human person/community rather than communion within Godself. LaCugna's main argument is that we should focus on the economic Trinity, God *pro nobis* or for us rather than God *in se* or in Godself, but she notes that "the temptation will be to reify the idea of community by positing an intradivine 'community' or society of persons that exists alongside, or above, the human community."[47] LaCugna defines the Spirit as "the animating power of the economy, making God's will and work known and realized in Jesus Christ and in each one of us. The Spirit humanizes God, and also divinizes human beings, making persons theonomous and catholic."[48] LaCugna points out that the experience of *koinonia* (community/communion) in the Spirit is one that upholds the uniqueness of the individual. She states:

> *Koinonia* does not swallow up the individual, nor obscure his or her uniqueness and unique contribution, nor take away individual freedom by assimilating it into a collective will. The goal of Christian community, constituted by the Spirit in union with Jesus Christ, is to provide a place in which *everyone* is accepted as an ineffable, unique, and unrepeatable image of God.[49]

---

[45] Ibid., 1. On Jesus as the revelation of what it means to be a person, see 292–96; on the Holy Spirit as the principle of communion, see 296–300.

[46] For a description of the key factors of what it means to be person for LaCugna based on the understanding of person given by the Trinity, see ibid., 288–92.

[47] Ibid., 15.

[48] Ibid., 296. *Theonomous* means subject to or governed by God, but in an internal sense in which God's law is written on our hearts.

[49] Ibid., 299. Miroslav Volf takes a similar approach to the concerns of postmodernism (see "The Trinity Is Our Social Program: The Doctrine of the Trinity and the Shape of Social Engagement," *Modern Theology* 14 [1998]: 403–23). The social analogy of the Trinity becomes a means of protecting the identity of the other in the face of the totalizing effect of the metanarrative (408). Volf does argue, however, that we should not model our relationships on God's Trinitarian love, which is a reciprocal love, but rather should model our relationships on God's love for the world that is "deeply flawed" and "suffused with enmity" (413).

We only become individuals in and through relationship and community.

Encountering Mystery: Love as Source, Word, and Spirit

One can escape the linguistic trap of Persons in communion by using a trinitarian image of God as Love. Love offers a better analogue than Person because it is the essence of relationality. Pure relationality is what enables existence. Because all existence finds its ground and being and sustenance in God as Love, being is always already relational. The source of being or our existence is relationality, that is, love.

While LaCugna's attempt to use the Trinity to redefine the common concept of person is laudable, the problem is that it is very difficult for the contemporary mind to think "person" and not "individual." LaCugna herself notes this danger:

> We in the west today think of a person as a "self" who may be further defined as a center of consciousness, a free, intentional subject, one who knows and is known, loves and is loved, an individual identity, a unique personality endowed with certain rights, a moral agent, someone who experiences, weighs, decides, and acts. This fits well with the idea that God is personal, but not at all with the idea that God is three persons. Three persons defined in this way would amount to three gods, three beings who act independently, three conscious individuals.[50]

While LaCugna wants to conform the common notion of person to the Trinity, it is the opposite that occurs. When people hear the Trinity described as three Persons in communion, they conform the Trinity to their notion of person as an individual in relationship with another individual, thus leading to the very misconception of Trinity that LaCugna warns about in the passage above.

LaCugna is critical of a trinitarian theology that follows Augustine in conceiving of God as "individual consciousness and its internal differentiations," because it leads to a focus on the individual and his

---

[50] LaCugna, *God for Us*, 250.

or her journey inward in introspection and self-reflection.[51] Augustine models the Trinity on the human soul as memory, understanding, and will, drawing on the idea that we are created in the image and likeness of God, an idea that has been critiqued by LaCugna, among others. However, if one understands human consciousness in a new way given contemporary study in the field of phenomenology, then consciousness becomes a journey of intentionality (being directed outward beyond oneself) and intersubjectivity (our inherent relationality) rather than a solipsistic or self-centered turning inward on oneself.[52] There can be no self-reflection without relationship to and with another. This understanding of personhood and human consciousness is manifest in the gospel witness to Jesus Christ as one who ultimately lives and dies for the other.

LaCugna's dismissal of the Augustinian tradition of God as one consciousness throws us back to a misconception of Trinity as three consciousnesses that then leads to a conception of God as three individuals. The issue is not the oneness of consciousness, a point LaCugna does not dispute. Rather, the issue is the understanding of consciousness as able to exist individually and independently rather than as interrelated and intersubjective. We can sidestep the entire question by moving from "person" to "love" as the primary analogy of understanding the Trinity.

LaCugna's own focus on the experience and revelation of God in the economy of salvation supports the claim of this work that one comes to know the meaning of person and community not in God's inner life, but rather in the relationship between God and humanity that is revealed in the incarnate Word and the Spirit-filled community. Her focus on *oikonomia* (economy), God's plan of creation and salvation, results in a redefinition of *person* that is revealed in the incarnation

---

[51] Ibid., 247.

[52] LaCugna does acknowledge this phenomenological understanding of person in her critique of Barth and Rahner (ibid., 251) and in her section on John MacMurray (ibid., 251ff.). The problem with LaCugna's use of MacMurray is that he is talking about God as personal in that God acts, not God as three personal others or three agents of action. In this sense MacMurray's conception of God fits better with the image put forth in this book where the Son and Spirit disclose God as Love revealed and enacted in the economy. See also Heidi Russell, *The Heart of Rahner: The Theological Implications of Andrew Tallon's Theory of Triune Consciousness*, Marquette Studies in Theology 64 (Milwaukee: Marquette University Press, 2009), 234.

of Christ. The understanding of what it means to be person as for-another and from-another comes from the Incarnation of Love, the self-revelation and self-manifestation of God in the world as human. Thus we understand our human personhood in Christ as having its ground and existence in love and its essence in relationality. To exist is to be in relation because we have been loved into existence.

LaCugna does not acknowledge that this new definition of inter-related and inclusive personhood exemplified in Jesus is the self-communication of God *in a human person.*[53] Jesus as human, not the Triune Persons, is the exemplar of personhood for human beings, a point that LaCugna herself highlights.[54] To understand what it means to be a human person in communion with God and one another, we do not look to the inner relations of the Trinity, but to God incarnate in the human person of Jesus of Nazareth. Jesus reveals divinized humanity, Love incarnate, to us. The Word of God is person in the modern, psychological sense of the word as an individual being or subject with a center of consciousness and freedom, only in and through union with humanity in Jesus Christ.

Likewise, the appropriate understanding of communion or community is not found in the intra-divine relations among the Three in the Trinity, but rather in the community formed by the presence of the Holy Spirit as witnessed in scripture. The Spirit is Love enacted and unfolded in the world. LaCugna wants to move away from any talk of intradivine community and focus on the Spirit working in and through

---

[53] There are theological debates about whether the persona or hypostasis of Jesus is divine or human. The Second Council of Constantinople affirms that the person, the bearer of the divine and human nature, is divine. One must again recognize that the word *persona* that is being used in these debates does not carry the meaning of a psychological center of consciousness and freedom that the word means today. The Third Council of Constantinople affirms that Jesus had to have a fully human will and center of action; thus, the connotations of the word *person* today are what the councils affirm of Jesus's humanity. When I use *person* in reference to Jesus, I am referring to Jesus as a human being as opposed to his being "hypostasized" or individualized in the divine Person of the Logos. In the Rahnerian sense that human nature is the *capax Dei,* we see that in Jesus what it means to be human is perfectly fulfilled. To be a human person is to be one whose potential is fulfilled in that it is grounded in God as love and becomes the manifestation of that love in the world.

[54] LaCugna, *God for Us*, 292.

human beings in a way that brings them into *koinonia* (community/communion) while preserving the uniqueness that makes them individuals. The individuality and individual freedom that LaCugna seeks to preserve in the human notion of community is precisely the reason this image does not work as a metaphor for the trinitarian Persons, where the notions of individuality and individual freedom must be excluded. LaCugna is seeking a metaphor that allows these notions to exist within a human community while at the same time negating the overemphasis on individuality in the current culture that has led to a breakdown of community. Focusing on the Trinity as Love enables one to make that corrective. The Spirit-filled community witnessed in scripture is one in which a radical equality and mutuality occur, or at least are held as the ideal, so that there is no longer Jew nor Gentile, slave nor free, male nor female (Gal 3:28).

In addressing the concern that the Trinity protect the distinctness and otherness of persons in community, Jean-Luc Marion's insight can be used to note the necessity of distance between giver and gift.[55] Marion's sense of exchange always requires maintaining a distance that can never be crossed.[56] "With love," Marion explains, "it is a matter of the other as such, irreducibly distinct and autonomous. If I were somehow to appropriate this other for myself, I would first have to reduce it to the rank of a slave, of an animal object, and thus lose it as other."[57] Love and relationship requires that the other remain other. Love does not possess or control the other. Love engenders freedom in the other, allowing that other to be other than I. Love creates and enables distinction while bridging separation. Like the Trinity in the theology of Maximus the Confessor, love holds diversity without opposition and unity that does not remove distinction. In order to understand being persons in communion, we follow LaCugna's lead and look to the way in which the Spirit is the action of God in each of us, making us persons in the way that Jesus is person. To be a person as Jesus is person is to be for another and from another, God revealed as Love in the world. God as Love continues to be unfolded in the world as Spirit in and through human persons and the bonds

---

[55] Jean-Luc Marion, *God without Being: Hors-Texte*, trans. Thomas A. Carlson, 2nd ed. (Chicago: University of Chicago Press, 2012), 104.

[56] Ibid.

[57] Jean-Luc Marion, *Prolegomena to Charity*, trans. Stephen E. Lewis (New York: Fordham University Press, 2002), 75.

of love that create true communion among humankind, creation, and God. This Spirit of Love is the catalyst for authentic social change, combatting oppression and fighting injustice in the world. Spirit-filled persons continue to bear witness, following in the footsteps of the first Christian martyrs, giving up even their own existence for the sake of Love, for the sake of the other whom the world does not recognize as human or person.

At best, LaCugna's critics fault her for ambiguity in maintaining some concept of immanent Trinity to protect the freedom of God and refrain from making God dependent on creation.[58] At worst, they fault her for an annihilation of God's freedom and a total conflation of the immanent Trinity into the economy of salvation.[59] By shifting from Person to Source, Word, and Spirit of Love, one can talk about an immanent Trinity that is revealed in the economy of salvation, but without abandoning language of God *in se* altogether. The revelation of the economic Trinity (God acting in creation and salvation) does in fact reveal to us God's very self, the immanent Trinity. What is revealed is God as Love manifested and enacted in human history. The economic Trinity does not simply reveal God. It reveals God in relation to humanity. Following LaCugna's principle of focusing on *oikonomia* (economy, meaning God's plan of creation and salvation) and letting *oikonomia* inform *theologia* (the mystery of God), the economic Trinity reveals the immanent Trinity. Who God is in relation to us is not other than who God is in Godself. God is revealed as Love, the Unoriginate Source of Love, the revealed Word of Love, and the enacted Spirit of Love. Using the analogy of Love protects the mystery of God *in se*, in that Love is unfathomable, inexhaustible, and incomprehensible—something we experience but in a way that eludes our cognitive grasp. To recall Marion's terms, Love is an icon that opens the incomprehensible in such a way that allows us to talk about *theologia*, God *in se*, the immanent Trinity, but in a way that

---

[58] Kärkkäinen, *The Trinity*, 187–93. While Kärkkäinen notes the ambiguity in LaCugna's position and the many times in which she states that there is a role for *theologia* in protecting the mystery of God and that God cannot be reduced to our experience of God, he nonetheless concludes, "In sum, it seems to me that the end result of LaCugna's program is the collapse of the immanent Trinity into the economic" (191).

[59] See Paul Molnar, *Divine Freedom and the Doctrine of the Immanent Trinity* (New York: T & T Clark, 2002).

is grounded in our experience of God who has revealed Godself as Love in the economy of salvation. Love preserves the mystery of God *in se* without denying God's revelation of self. As an icon, face, gift, the analogy of Love protects the otherness of God, and therefore the freedom and hiddenness of God *in se*. Contrary to the arguments that LaCugna cites from Piet Schoonenberg that God's offer to humanity requires a free acceptance, and thereby brings about "a new way of being both for God and for the creature,"[60] Marion explains that love gains nothing from its reception or lack thereof.[61] God's offer does not bring about a new way of being for God. Rather, that offer reveals who God is eternally in Godself, that is, Love. This image of the immanent Trinity as Love protects God's independence and freedom from creation, while remaining true to who God has revealed Godself to be in relation to creation in the economy of salvation.

LaCugna concludes in an uncanny synchronicity with Jean-Luc Marion, "Love creates new being; love brings into existence anything and everything that is. Without love nothing would be at all. Apart from love there is only nonbeing which is the same as nonpersonhood."[62] In a footnote to this passage, LaCugna uses the example of suicide, and ultimately any death, to note that ceasing to exist bodily is not the same as ceasing to exist entirely, because existence continues when one is remembered and loved in a network of relationships.[63] She goes on to connect this sense of existence to eternal existence in light of God as "the one who 'remembers' everyone and everything."[64]

LaCugna's theology ultimately ends up in mystery and praise. Part of LaCugna's emphasis on God as Person is an understanding of person as "ineffable: an inexhaustible mystery that is not fully 'communicable' to another."[65] One must raise the question of using this definition to then speak of three Persons in the Trinity, if one is going to hold to the

---

[60] LaCugna, *God for Us*, 219, citing Piet Schoonenberg, "Trinity—the Consummated Covenant: Theses on the Doctrine of the Trinitarian God," *Studies in Religion* 5 (1975–76): 114.

[61] Marion, *God without Being*, 47; Marion, *The Erotic Phenomenon*, 71–73.

[62] LaCugna, *God for Us*, 265, see also 301, 303.

[63] Ibid., 309–10n75. Note that death and suicide are also important topics for Marion in both *The Erotic Phenomenon* and *Prolegomena to Charity.*

[64] Ibid., 310n75.

[65] Ibid., 289.

Nicene understanding of *homoousios* (of the same being). For LaCugna, "the ultimate predicate of incomprehensibility is 'person.' . . . Person is at root a term of apophasis or negation; by predicating personhood of someone we acknowledge their indefinability and ineffable mystery."[66] God as ineffable, inexhaustible mystery leads to silence and praise. Ultimately all talk of God as Trinity leads back to God as holy mystery before whom we fall silent in praise and adoration.[67]

Mystery is not the antithesis of revelation. It is what has been revealed. LaCugna states:

> We do not say that God is mystery because we know nothing about God. As a partner in love, God permanently remains Mystery to us, no matter how advanced is our intimacy. Like all love relationships, the involvement between God and humanity cannot be easily described and can only be inadequately explained.[68]

For LaCugna, God is mystery *because* God is personal. The more we come to know God, the deeper we enter into that relationship, the more we encounter mystery. That mystery of love encompasses us as we fall into the infinite depths of God. LaCugna explains, "The more intimate our knowledge of another, the more we are drawn to that person's unique mystery, and the deeper that mystery becomes."[69] There is always more to another person than we can possibly know, just as the more we come to know God, the more we know God as mystery. We experience a congruence between the finite infinity of the human other and the Infinite Infinity of the divine Other, and in that experience, we recognize and name God as Love, Unoriginate Source revealed in Word and enacted in Spirit.

Unfolding Catholicity

All language falls short of capturing the infinity and the incomprehensibility of God. The analogue of God as Unoriginate Source of

---

[66] Ibid., 302.

[67] See Karen Kilby, "Is an Apophatic Trinitarianism Possible?" *International Journal of Systematic Theology* 12 (2010): 65–77.

[68] LaCugna, *God for Us*, 323.

[69] Ibid., 321.

Love revealed in the Word and enacted in the Spirit is an image that both opens one to the mystery and ineffability of God and addresses the legitimate concerns of the social trinitarians. The social trinitarians raise several important issues to be addressed by trinitarian theology, such as the need for a greater emphasis on intersubjectivity and community. The social trinitarians make an effort to redefine what is meant by person by hearkening to the relation of the Persons of the Trinity. The danger in addressing these concerns through the image of Trinity as a fellowship or community of Persons is the danger of misconceiving such language as tritheism. Such concerns, however, can be addressed when one comes to understand what it means to be person in and through the person of Jesus Christ, the incarnate revelation of God as Love in the world.

In the person of Jesus one sees a person whose origin is Love itself. He exists as a human person in mutual and equal relationships and expresses his own identity in relationship with others and in giving himself in love for others. Thus we come to know that being person means being relational and intersubjective in and through the revelation of Love incarnate in the human person of Jesus the Christ. Likewise, the concept of community as interrelationships based on mutuality and equality giving rise to a society that operates in a manner that is just and loving does not need the tritheistic image of a society or fellowship of three Persons in the Trinity to be grounded in trinitarian theology. Rather, when one understands the Trinity as God as Love in Source, Word, and Spirit, the Spirit is the principle of Love enacted in the world, a principle that is illustrated in the theological concept of the body of Christ.

Our catholicity is experienced and expressed when we become this unfolding of the wholeness of Love in the world. The Spirit creates and unites the community in this Love that does not create uniformity but rather creates the space and openness that empowers the authentic diversity that is necessary for community, allowing each person to unfold as his or her own subwhole. The recognition of the indwelling Spirit in each person creates the bonds of mutuality and equality necessary for a healthy society. Such community that is created in and through the Spirit finds its origin in Love and recognizes that persons come to be only in loving relationship to another. Our understanding of personhood and society should be grounded in our understanding of God as Trinity, but that understanding need not lead to tritheistic images of God. God as Love is revealed in the incarnate Christ who reveals to us what it means to be a human person, an image that is enfolded in each of us. God as Love is enacted and unfolded in the Holy Spirit. The Spirit is the dynamism and power that creates community and forms it to be the body of Christ, the ongoing revelation of God as Love in the world as a catalyst for social change, working to overcome oppression and injustice. We are created and have our existence in that Unoriginate Source of Love and are called to unfold our personhood in the enfolded image of the incarnate Love that is Jesus Christ in and through the power of the Spirit of Love that dwells and acts within each of us, bringing us into communion with God and one another.

Chapter 7

Conclusion: Catholicity = Wholeness of Love

When we understand the Trinity in light of David Bohm's model of wholeness recast in the analogy of Love, we discover the wholeness of Love expressed through the Word of Love that is enfolded into all of creation. That wholeness of Love is then unfolded into the world through the power of the Holy Spirit in what might be called catholicity. Catholicity is an orientation toward wholeness, and that wholeness is the Source of Love that is expressed in the Word and enacted in the Spirit. John Haughey asks, "What does the Trinity do when it is off work? It ones."[1] One might also say that it "wholes." The Trinity wholes through love. The Source of All Love enfolds and unfolds Love in the world through the Word and Spirit. We are called to participate in the wholeness of the Trinity and in the work of enfolding and unfolding Love in the world.

To participate in that work is to shift from a culture of individuality and competition to a vision of an interconnected whole. As we have seen in the new physics, that interconnectedness is woven into the foundations of creation itself. The patristic theologians envisioned creation through the Logos in such a way that the Logos or Mind of God became the ordering principle of the world. In light of the new discoveries of the nonlocal connectedness of the subatomic world, we can envision that the relationality of Triune Love is enfolded into

[1] John Haughey, *A Biography of the Spirit: There Lies the Dearest Freshness Deep Down Things* (Maryknoll, NY: Orbis Books, 2015), entry for Oct. 30.

creation on a molecular level. It is at the core of what it means to exist. Love and connectedness ground existence.

The Crucifixion in a Fragmented World

As David Bohm explains, fragmentation is at the root of some of our deepest self-destructive tendencies as human beings. Instead of unfolding the wholeness of Love in the world, in our egos we cling to division, choosing self over other, nation over globe, race over humanity. Ilia Delio notes:

> We are the most uncatholic species; we prefer self-interest over the interest of others, the law over the spirit, sowing where we do not reap and condemning without mercy. If nature is an evolving whole, the human person is constantly threatening to destroy the whole. This is sin: consciously to disrupt or sever what is otherwise part of the whole.[2]

She goes on to proclaim Jesus's life and ministry as the antidote to this fragmentation through his expression of love as whole-making through healing, through forgiveness, and ultimately through his death and resurrection.

Our lives are only complete in death. In our death, the person we have become over the course of our lifetime becomes definitive. Likewise, Jesus's absolute and infinite yes to God that is who he is as the incarnation of God's Word of Love becomes definitive in his death by crucifixion. Death is the culmination of life. Crucifixion is the culmination of Jesus's life, his ministry, and his actions. Jesus living out who he is, which is to say, the revelation of God as Love in the world, leads to his crucifixion. Jesus remains true to what he professes, to who he is even to death. In a world of fragmentation, alienation, and division, Jesus not only preaches the wholeness of Love, he incarnates it. He believes that his death will be vindicated, that something definitive will be accomplished through his death, but at the same time he experiences uncertainty and fear in death. That experience of uncertainty and fear in death is part of humanity,

[2] Ilia Delio, *Making All Things New: Catholicity, Cosmology, Consciousness* (Maryknoll, NY: Orbis Books, 2015), 77.

part of Jesus's inability to know with certainty that is part of what it means to be human.

In the crucifixion we see God's solidarity with humanity even at that point where we experience the absence of God. Even at that point where we feel most isolated and cut off from all of our interconnectedness with God and others, God's Word of Love is expressed. Jesus Emmanuel, God-with-us, cries out with us and for us in our fragmentation and alienation, "My God, my God, why have you abandoned me?" Jesus voices our longing for wholeness in the midst of our deepest divisions and separations. Jesus's unconditional yes to God persists even in the face of his own human lack of comprehension of God's plan. His loving and obedient surrender to God on the cross is humanity's response to God's offer. In Christ is our acceptance of God as Love. In Christ is our acceptance of wholeness and our interconnectedness that can be the source of both our deepest joy and our deepest pain. Our finite and partial yes is joined to his unconditional and absolute yes. Jesus says yes for us when we ourselves cannot or will not.

God's wrath does not crucify Jesus; human sinfulness does. The cross is not about God demanding satisfaction for human sins. The cross is humanity's response to the revelation of God as Love in the world. The cross is the choosing of fragmentation over wholeness, alienation over interconnectedness. In *Crossing the Threshold of Hope*, Saint John Paul II writes:

> In a certain sense one could say that *confronted with our human freedom, God decided to make himself "impotent."* And one could say that God is paying for the great gift bestowed upon a being He created "in his image, after his likeness" (cf. Gn 1:26). Before this gift, He remains consistent, and *places Himself before the judgment of man*, before an illegitimate tribunal which asks Him provocative questions: "Then you are a king?" (cf. Jn 18:37); "Is it true that all which happens in the world, in the history of Israel, in the history of all nations, depends on you?" We know Christ's response to this question before Pilate's tribunal: "For this I was born and for this I came into the world, to testify to the truth" (Jn 18:37). But then: "What is truth?" (Jn 18:38), and here ended the judicial proceeding, that tragic proceeding in which man accused God before the tribunal of his own history, and in which the sentence handed down did

> not conform to the truth. Pilate says: "I find no guilt in him" (Jn 18:38), and a second later he orders: "Take him yourselves and crucify him!" (Jn 19:6). In this way he washes his hands of the issue and returns the responsibility to the violent crowd. Therefore, *the condemnation of God by man is not based on truth, but on arrogance, on an underhanded conspiracy.* Isn't this the truth about the history of humanity, the truth about our century? In our time the same condemnation has been repeated in many courts of totalitarian regimes.[3]

Every time we fail to see what is sacred, fail to give reverence and respect to what is sacred, we are guilty of the very sinfulness that led the people of Jesus's time to crucify him. We fail to unfold the Love and wholeness that is at the core of creation. When we look at the world through the lens of fragmentation and alienation instead of wholeness, catholicity, and love, we fail to see God as Love expressed and enacted in the Word and Spirit. Every time in our own lives we fail to recognize and respond to Love in our midst, we crucify Christ. We crucify Christ in our blindness or apathy toward the suffering of the innocent. We crucify Christ when we refuse to see creation as an interconnected whole. The cross is our false judgment of God—a judgment not based on truth, but on our ego, our arrogance and underhanded conspiracy, our attempts to protect the status quo, to maintain our power and control—in a word, what we call sin. Our judgment is based on individuality and competition rather than our interconnectedness. Pilate asks, "What is truth?" One might as well ask, "What is love?" In the passion narrative Pilate does not recognize Love when it is right in front of him. Peter denies Love. Judas betrays Love. Like Pilate, we fail to recognize Love. Like Peter and Judas, we deny and betray Love. We live "uncatholic" lives of division rather than interconnection, and in doing so, we fail to see the Love that is enfolded in creation. We fail to unfold the Love of God in the world.

Even in our failures, however, the cross is not about anger; it is about Love revealed. The cross is not God substituting punishment of Jesus for punishment of us. The good news of Easter is that God's reaction to our sinfulness is not wrathful punishment, but rather to embrace it in a willing acceptance of the cross and to redeem it

[3] John Paul II, *Crossing the Threshold of Hope* (New York: Knopf, 2005), 65.

through an outpouring of love for us in the resurrection. Sin is not overcome by wrath; it is overcome by Love. God brings resurrection out of our crucifixions of God. In that response is the forgiveness of our sins—that God looks at us and sees us for who we truly are (sees the truth). God sees all that we have done and failed to do, and loves us unconditionally. God enters into solidarity with us, into union with us, and draws us into the divine embrace of the Trinity. God's reaction to human sinfulness is not anger and wrath. God's response is the gift of self, and that self is unconditional love and forgiveness. God as Love expresses Godself in the Word and enacts that Love in the Spirit.

Unfolding Love

It is in union with Christ that we are able to join our partial and finite yes to Christ's complete and infinite yes. Christ is both the offer of God as Love in the world and humanity's acceptance of that offer. In Christ and the Spirit, the God of Love is God for us. Elizabeth Johnson has a wonderful and simple formula for the Trinity that captures this image of the Trinity—God beyond us, God with us, and God within us.[4] God as Love is Word and Spirit, so that God can become "Love for us." It is of the very nature of God to go outside of Godself. That is what love is, a going outward to what is other. God's love is freely given, though, so we must be careful not to place any necessity on God. At the same time we have to acknowledge that freedom and gratuity mean something different in the context of love. Love must be truly free, and at the same time love compels one in certain ways. Freedom in the context of love is not understood as the ability to do whatever I want. I freely act for the good of my loved one, but in a way, love also compels that action. The action flows out of my love, while still being freely chosen.

It is the Spirit that enacts and unfolds Love in the world by uniting us to Christ and to one another. In the Spirit we become community, the body of Christ. In the Spirit we live out the interconnectedness that is who we are at the core of our created being. In the Spirit we become catholic. Being among the baptized does not mean that God somehow loves us more than anyone else. God loves all humanity and

[4] Elizabeth Johnson, *Quest for the Living God* (New York: Continuum, 2007), 204–5.

creation itself unconditionally. Being baptized means we are called to be a member of the body of Christ. Being baptized means we are to allow the Spirit to unfold God as Love for the world in and through our lives and community. As the body of Christ we are called to be the ongoing expression of God's Word of Love in the world. Ilia Delio echoes that call in her invocation to birth Christ in the world:

> Get up! Go into the world and live in the flow of love. Forgive, show mercy, be compassionate, care for the poor, tend to the earth as family; find your inner wholeness in the love of God and create new wholes in your midst, in your communities, your workplaces, at shopping malls, and jazz fests. Live in the energy of the Spirit; let yourself be led into new patterns of wholeness, into new structures and languages that kindle life more abundantly.[5]

One sees an example of such living the flow of love in Rwandan native Marcel Uwineza, SJ. In a recent article in *America*, Uwineza recalls his experience twenty years ago of the Rwandan genocide in which his parents, brothers, and sister were killed. These killings emerged out of the tribal fragmentation that was encouraged and fostered under Western colonial rule. Yet Uwineza recounts the hope found in the martyrdom of a group of young people in secondary school who refused to separate themselves along ethnic lines when militiamen attacked their school in 1997, three years after the genocide.[6] Thirteen of the students were killed in the attack. Uwineza's own moment of reconciled interconnectedness came in an encounter with one of the people who had killed his siblings:

> One day I met one of the killers of my brothers and sister. Upon seeing me, he came toward me. I thought he was coming to kill me too. But I could not believe what happened. As if in a movie, he knelt before me and asked me to forgive him. After a time of confusion, asking myself what was happening, and by a force which I could not describe, I took him, embraced him

---

[5] Delio, *Making All Things New*, 190.

[6] Marcel Uwineza, "On Christian Hope: What Makes It Distinctive and Credible?" *America* 214, no. 11 (April 4–11, 2016): 26.

> and said: "I forgive you; the Lord has been good to me." Ever since that moment, I have felt free.[7]

He speaks of how the healing he experienced in forgiveness has enabled him to heal others. The Holy Spirit as the Love enacted unfolded the wholeness of love in and through him.

In a *Time* magazine blog Iranian Maryam Bighash writes of living in France and being attacked by young Muslim men when walking home from middle school wearing a cross. She is now a student at Wheaton College in the United States. When her Christian professor was placed on administrative leave for wearing a hijab, Bighash decided to don one of her own in solidarity:

> On Dec. 17, after Dr. Hawkins was placed on administrative leave, I wore a hijab to continue her message. After breakfast on my way to class, I left the cafeteria and approached the foyer doorway. As I walked through the door frame, a young male classmate in front me noticed my hijab. Thinking he was holding the door for me, I naively walked through the door only to feel a thud against my face after he forcefully swung the hinged metal toward me and chuckled. I walked away numb. I wondered if I was Christian enough for Wheaton College, and part of me wanted to hate those around me. But then I was reminded of Jesus' teachings and Dr. Hawkins' example: self-sacrificial love of the other, as modeled in the life of Jesus.
>
> Sometimes I wonder if I love Muslims too much to live in a Christian community. Yet I also sometimes feel too Christian to be accepted by Muslims. What I do know is that Jesus loves both communities equally, and that is why I have chosen to support Dr. Hawkins. I hope the administration of Wheaton College will allow the students and the faculty to model Jesus's teachings, without qualifications.[8]

Uwineza and Bighash offer prophetic witness to us of what it means to be catholic, to live in the wholeness of love. They show

[7] Ibid., 24.

[8] Maryam Bighash, "Wheaton Student: I Wore a Hijab to Continue the Professor's Message," *Time* (January 12, 2016).

how unfolding the wholeness of Love in the world through the Spirit of Christ that is enfolded within them means overcoming fragmentation and division.

Our world is torn apart by ethnic and racial violence, by interreligious violence, and by political violence. In the midst of a presidential primary election in the United States we hear candidates for the highest office in our land spew vitriol and hatred in the public forum under the masquerade of political debate. Our ability to understand diversity as a prerequisite for unity and the need to allow space for the other to be other in order to be in relationship is in jeopardy. At this time of division and fragmentation, the prophetic voices recall for us what it means to be the body of Christ, the sacramental sign of God as Love incarnate in the world.

The Call of Pope Francis

Pope Francis has called on the church to live out its catholicity, its wholeness in love. He warns that the economy and culture of consumerism create fragmentation in our world that must be opposed by catholicity. In his apostolic exhortation *Evangelii Gaudium (The Joy of the Gospel)* Pope Francis entreats us to say no to an economy of exclusion and asks:

> How can it be that it is not a news item when an elderly homeless person dies of exposure, but it is news when the stock market loses two points? This is a case of exclusion. Can we continue to stand by when food is thrown away while people are starving? This is a case of inequality. Today everything comes under the laws of competition and the survival of the fittest, where the powerful feed upon the powerless. As a consequence, masses of people find themselves excluded and marginalized: without work, without possibilities, without any means of escape. (*EG,* no. 53)

He warns that the answer to this fragmentation and exclusion is not going to be found in the free market. Rather, that system that creates such a disparity between rich and poor anesthetizes us to the suffering of others deepening the fragmentation. He prophesies:

> In this context, some people continue to defend trickle-down theories which assume that economic growth, encouraged by a free market, will inevitably succeed in bringing about greater justice and inclusiveness in the world. This opinion, which has never been confirmed by the facts, expresses a crude and naive trust in the goodness of those wielding economic power and in the sacralized workings of the prevailing economic system. Meanwhile, the excluded are still waiting. To sustain a lifestyle which excludes others, or to sustain enthusiasm for that selfish ideal, a globalization of indifference has developed. Almost without being aware of it, we end up being incapable of feeling compassion at the outcry of the poor, weeping for other people's pain, and feeling a need to help them, as though all this were someone else's responsibility and not our own. The culture of prosperity deadens us; we are thrilled if the market offers us something new to purchase. In the meantime all those lives stunted for lack of opportunity seem a mere spectacle; they fail to move us. (*EG,* no. 54)

Our interconnectedness means that when one part of the body suffers, the whole body suffers. Pope Francis notes that inequality leads to outbreaks of violence that will not be eliminated without the elimination of injustice (*EG,* no. 59).

Part of the response on the part of the church to these challenges is a living out of our interconnectedness in relationship. We are called to unfold the wholeness of Love. Pope Francis suggests:

> The Gospel tells us constantly to run the risk of a face-to-face encounter with others, with their physical presence which challenges us, with their pain and their pleas, with their joy which infects us in our close and continuous interaction. True faith in the incarnate Son of God is inseparable from self-giving, from membership in the community, from service, from reconciliation with others. The Son of God, by becoming flesh, summoned us to the revolution of tenderness. (*EG,* no. 88)

We overcome the isolation and individualism so rampant in our world through caring communion with one another. Pope Francis suggests that the healing of our world can only be found in

> a fraternal love capable of seeing the sacred grandeur of our neighbour, of finding God in every human being, of tolerating the nuisances of life in common by clinging to the love of God, of opening the heart to divine love and seeking the happiness of others just as their heavenly Father does. (*EG,* no. 92)

In a world of division, fragmentation, and violence, the pope asks that in our own Christian communities we do not give into such temptation. He pleads:

> I especially ask Christians in communities throughout the world to offer a radiant and attractive witness of fraternal communion. Let everyone admire how you care for one another, and how you encourage and accompany one another: "By this everyone will know that you are my disciples, if you have love for one another" (Jn 13:35). This was Jesus's heartfelt prayer to the Father: "That they may all be one . . . in us . . . so that the world may believe" (Jn 17:21). (*EG,* no. 99)

In this way the wholeness of Love that is expressed in the person of Christ and has been enfolded into creation can be unfolded in the world through the Spirit-filled body of Christ. This communion must first and foremost be expressed through the inclusion of and solidarity with the poor, if it is to be true (*EG,* nos. 186–92). To realize truly the interconnectedness at the core of our being, we must first address the gaping wounds in the body. We encounter God as Source of Love when we encounter that Word of Love expressed and living among the least of us.

In words that seem to echo physicist Lee Smolin, Pope Francis proclaims that in striving to transform the world through solidarity and love, "time is greater than space" (*EG,* no. 222). He goes on to explain:

> One of the faults which we occasionally observe in sociopolitical activity is that spaces and power are preferred to time and processes. Giving priority to space means madly attempting to keep everything together in the present, trying to possess all the spaces of power and of self-assertion; it is to crystallize processes and presume to hold them back. Giving priority to time means being concerned about initiating processes rather than possessing spaces. Time governs spaces, illumines them

> and makes them links in a constantly expanding chain, with no possibility of return. What we need, then, is to give priority to actions which generate new processes in society and engage other persons and groups who can develop them to the point where they bear fruit in significant historical events. Without anxiety, but with clear convictions and tenacity. (*EG,* no. 223)

We work in the context of community. No one person or country accomplishes it all. I cannot be the body of Christ by myself. I can only be the body of Christ in union with my brothers and sisters, neighbors and strangers all in union with Christ the head. In that context of community the world can be changed. But change happens over time, and the fact that change does not occur all at once cannot be an excuse for doing nothing. Each of us in our own individual contexts must be open to the Spirit working within us and through our communities to unfold God's Love in a unique way, but in a way that is part of a bigger whole through our interconnectedness across time and history.

In his most recent encyclical, *Laudato Si' (On Care for Our Common Home),* Pope Francis continues his themes of our interconnectedness and particular care for the poor in the context of all of creation. Having examined the ways in which humanity has become a force of destruction in the created world, the pope calls for an "integral ecology." In words that again echo physicists David Bohm and Lee Smolin, Pope Francis maintains:

> It cannot be emphasized enough how everything is interconnected. Time and space are not independent of one another, and not even atoms or subatomic particles can be considered in isolation. Just as the different aspects of the planet—physical, chemical and biological—are interrelated, so too living species are part of a network which we will never fully explore and understand. A good part of our genetic code is shared by many living beings. It follows that the fragmentation of knowledge and the isolation of bits of information can actually become a form of ignorance, unless they are integrated into a broader vision of reality. (*LS,* no. 138)

An integral ecology takes into consideration the environmental, economic, and social concerns that cannot be addressed apart from one another (*LS,* nos. 137–42). Pope Francis's suggested responses to the crises of our time all center around the concept of dialogue, interdependence, community, and love.

Pope Francis grounds our interconnectedness and unity in creation itself. He maintains:

> The universe unfolds in God, who fills it completely. Hence, there is a mystical meaning to be found in a leaf, in a mountain trail, in a dewdrop, in a poor person's face. The ideal is not only to pass from the exterior to the interior to discover the action of God in the soul, but also to discover God in all things. Saint Bonaventure teaches us that "contemplation deepens the more we feel the working of God's grace within our hearts, and the better we learn to encounter God in creatures outside ourselves" [Bonaventure, II Sent., 23, 2, 3]. (*LS,* no. 233)

Like Bonaventure, Pope Francis grounds this connection between creation and God in the Trinity. In the incarnation the material world itself has been taken into God. In the Catholic sacramental tradition, material reality mediates our relationship to God and in that sacramental relationship, we experience not only our connectedness to God, but the interconnectedness of creation itself. Pope Francis exhorts:

> The Lord, in the culmination of the mystery of the Incarnation, chose to reach our intimate depths through a fragment of matter. He comes not from above, but from within, he comes that we might find him in this world of ours. In the Eucharist, fullness is already achieved; it is the living centre of the universe, the overflowing core of love and of inexhaustible life. Joined to the incarnate Son, present in the Eucharist, the whole cosmos gives thanks to God. Indeed the Eucharist is itself an act of cosmic love: "Yes, cosmic! Because even when it is celebrated on the humble altar of a country church, the Eucharist is always in some way celebrated on the altar of the world." The Eucharist joins heaven and earth; it embraces and penetrates all creation. The world which came forth from God's hands returns to him in blessed and undivided adoration: in the bread of the Eucharist, "creation is projected towards divinization, towards the holy wedding feast, towards unification with the Creator himself." Thus, the Eucharist is

> also a source of light and motivation for our concerns for the environment, directing us to be stewards of all creation. (*LS*, no. 237)[9]

Invoking the Trinity, he goes on to state,

> The Father is the ultimate source of everything, the loving and self-communicating foundation of all that exists. The Son, his reflection, through whom all things were created, united himself to this earth when he was formed in the womb of Mary. The Spirit, infinite bond of love, is intimately present at the very heart of the universe, inspiring and bringing new pathways. (*LS,* no. 238)

The Father is the Source of All Love that is enfolded into the world in creation and incarnation of the Word of Love and unfolded and enacted in the Spirit of Love. Relationship is at the heart of what it means to be created by a Triune God. Pope Francis summarizes:

> The divine Persons are subsistent relations, and the world, created according to the divine model, is a web of relationships. Creatures tend towards God, and in turn it is proper to every living being to tend towards other things, so that throughout the universe we can find any number of constant and secretly interwoven relationships. This leads us not only to marvel at the manifold connections existing among creatures, but also to discover a key to our own fulfilment. The human person grows more, matures more and is sanctified more to the extent that he or she enters into relationships, going out from themselves to live in communion with God, with others and with all creatures. In this way, they make their own that trinitarian dynamism which God imprinted in them when they were created. Everything is interconnected, and this invites us to develop a spirituality of that global solidarity which flows from the mystery of the Trinity. (*LS,* no. 240)

[9] The quotations are from John Paul II, *Ecclesia de Eucharistia* (April 17, 2003), 8; AAS 95 (2003), 438; and Benedict XVI, *Homily for the Mass of Corpus Domini* (June 15, 2006): AAS 98 (2006), 513, respectively.

From Lord to Love

As Pope Francis ends his apostolic exhortation and his encyclical with prayer, it seems appropriate to conclude with a reflection on how imaging God as Source of All Love enfolded and revealed in the Word and enacted in the Spirit has come to shape my own prayer life. One day, in the midst of all of this language about God as love, I found myself reading the psalms replacing the word *Lord* with *Love,* hearing Love both as a noun and a verb, hearing Love as an endearment.

To give a few examples from Sunday Evening Prayer I:

> Hurry LOVE! I call and call!
> Listen, I plead with you.
> Let my prayer rise like incense,
> my upraised hands like an evening sacrifice.
>
> LOVE, guard my lips,
> watch my every word.
> Let me never speak evil or consider hateful deeds,
> let me ever join the wicked to eat their lavish meals.
> (Ps. 141:1–4)

How does our understanding of these words shift when we start to imagine ourselves pleading with the Source of All Love, asking Love to hurry into our lives? What does it mean in our relationships to ask Love to guard our lips and watch our words?

> I pray, I plead, I cry for mercy, LOVE.
> There is no escape, so I turn to you LOVE.
> I know you are my refuge,
> all I have in the land of the living. (Ps. 142:5)

Again, what happens in our prayer when we feel ourselves pleading for mercy to the Source of All Love, turning to Love for our refuge?

Finally, we turn to the beautiful Philippians hymn, in which

> every tongue proclaim[s] to the glory of God our
> Father,
> Jesus Christ is LOVE. (Phil. 2:11)[10]

We proclaim that Jesus Christ is the Word of Love united to creation and expressed in the world.

Now as a caveat, I am not suggesting that these are good biblical translations or that they reflect the original author's intent. I am simply speaking to what it does to my image of God to change this word, how it changes my prayer life, my relationship to God, and ultimately, how it continues to change me. Because it does change me, little by little, day by day, and on some days more than others. Suddenly what had felt like an obligation and a burden feels like the most natural thing in the world. Suddenly the Christian moral life is not about following the law, to restate Paul's insight—it is about how I respond to being loved.

Living in relationship to the Triune God is about how we respond to the call to love more than we do now. Until I started changing the word *Lord* to *Love,* I had not realized the hidden resentment that I was feeling, the intuition that the word *Lord* meant power over, and that this "Lord" was someone who wanted to control me, someone I was supposed to obey. Had you asked me about my image of God, I would not have said any of that. I would have professed my belief in an all-loving God. Underneath, however, my independent spirit bristled at the concept of obeying my Lord. Unconsciously, I was responding as if my freedom and autonomy were in inverse rather than direct proportion to my dependence and obedience to God.

When I started to think, however, about what it means to obey Love, that resentment dropped away. In its place came a desire to do better, to be more, to be who I was created to be in unfolding the love that was enfolded into my heart in creation. Recently, James Doty, a neurosurgeon who also directs Stanford's Center for Compassion and Altruism Research and Education, was interviewed by Krista Tippett on her show, *On Being*. Doty spoke of the fact that our brains func-

---

[10] All three passages are taken from Linda Ekstrom, *Psalms for Morning and Evening Prayer* (Chicago: Liturgy Training Publications, 1995), 2–5.

tion differently when we meditate on love, or what he calls "open heartedness." Doty explained that by meditating on compassion, our fight-or-flight response actually diminishes (technically, the MRI shows that the amygdala shrinks).[11]

> In some ways, I guess you could say this is analogous to strengthening certain muscles and allowing others to atrophy. And, again, it shows you—and this is what I tell people—is that, just like muscles, our mental muscle, if you will, responds to exercise. It's just which exercise you're going to do. And one exercise relates to mindfulness, compassion, lovingkindness, having an open heart. And when you strengthen that muscle, the world becomes a vibrant place where you recognize the incredible aspect of humanity that surrounds you in every person, how every person has this incredible potential to change the world.
>
> Or you can do a form of exercise that makes you afraid, that makes you pull away, that makes you think that people are your enemies, or that people are out for something. And, unfortunately, sometimes it's an active choice, but for many people, they don't even understand that this is happening.[12]

We can choose to exercise the unfolding of love in our lives. I can meditate on a God who is Love, who has enfolded Godself as Love at the core of who I am and empowered me to participate in the unfolding of that Love in the world. Through that meditative prayer, we will come to better enact Love in the world. Our hearts can literally change our brains. Our altered brains will change our actions. That unfolding of love means I am empowered to live out my life in relationships that are loving, that engender mutuality and equality in the world.

With that recognition of what it means to live in love comes the recognition of my own constant failure, my own sinfulness, and my own need for mercy and forgiveness. This awareness of sin is not a scrupulous and shame-centered mindset, but rather the healthy guilt of being called to love more. Think about the story of the rich young man and his response to Jesus—"I have kept all these [commandments]." Jesus's response, though, to him and to me, is, "Go,

---

[11] "James Doty—The Magic Shop of the Brain," *On Being, with Krista Tippett*, February 11, 2016, available online.

[12] Ibid.

sell your possessions, and give the money to the poor, and you will have treasure in heaven; then come, follow me." Jesus's response is, be more, because I am not asking you to follow the law, I am asking you to follow me. Jesus asks us to give our lives over to love, to give up our lives for the sake of love.

That awes me. That makes me fall to my knees and realize that I can never do enough, and that I am loved anyway. The authentic saints often reflect on a sense of their own unworthiness and sinfulness, which initially seems puzzling, given the goodness of their lives. However, for many of them this sense of sin is not due to issues with scrupulosity; it is because they understand the call of love. And so now, when I don't hide from it or avoid it, I know the need for an examination of conscience that does not ask each day for a list of sins or an accounting of wrongdoing, but one that openly and honestly looks back at my day and asks, *Where could I have been more loving? Where did I fail to bother?* During Lent, Pope Francis asked the faithful not to fast from some favorite food or pastime, but rather to fast from indifference.[13] Herein lies the fast that deeply satisfies. Herein lies the truth of the words "I desire mercy, not sacrifice" (Mt 9:13), "I desire steadfast love and not sacrifice" (Hos 6:6).

These questions bring a deep humility in me and make me realize that worshiping the God who is Love, expressed and enacted in this world, following this God who is Love, demands far more from me than the God I called Lord. Yet doing so offers me such abundance of life and love in return that when I bother, when I heed that call to incarnate love in my own life, I find rewards in each and every moment far beyond what I could ever have imagined. And so I end these reflections with my own version of the priestly blessing from the Book of Numbers (6:24–26):

> May LOVE bless you and keep you;
> May LOVE's face shine upon you, and be gracious
>   to you;
> May LOVE's countenance be lifted up upon you, and
>   give you peace. (Nm 6:24–26)

---

[13] Christopher Hale, "Pope Francis' Guide to Lent: What You Should Give Up This Year," *Time*, February 18, 2015.

Bibliography

Albert, David Z. "Bohm's Alternative to Quantum Mechanics." *Scientific American* 270 (May 1994): 58–67.

Anatolios, Khaled. "The Influence of Irenaeus on Athanasius." In *Studia Patristica*, 463–76. Louvain: Peeters, 2001.

———. *Retrieving Nicaea: The Development and Meaning of Trinitarian Doctrine*. Grand Rapids, MI: Baker Academic, 2011.

———. "'When was God without Wisdom?': Trinitarian Hermeneutics and Rhetorical Strategy in Athanasius." In *Studia Patristica*, 117–23. Leuven: Peeters, 2006.

Anderson, Gary. "Introduction to Israelite Religion." In *The New Interpreter's Bible: A Commentary in Twelve Volumes*, edited by Leander Keck, David Petersen, et al. Volume 1, *Genesis to Leviticus,* 272–83. Nashville: Abingdon Press, 1994.

Ayres, Lewis. *Nicea and Its Legacy.* Oxford: Oxford University Press, 2004.

Boff, Leonardo. "Trinity." In *Mysterium Liberationis: Fundamental Concepts of Liberation Theology*, edited by Ignacio Ellacuría and Jon Sobrino, 389–403. Maryknoll, NY: Orbis Books, 1993.

———. *Trinity and Society*. Translated by Paul Burns. Maryknoll, NY: Orbis, 1988.

Bohm, David. "Dialogue on Science, Society, and the Generative Order." *Zygon* 25, no. 4 (December 1990): 449–67.

———. *The Essential David Bohm*. Edited by Lee Nichol. London: Routledge, 2003.

———. "Fragmentation and Wholeness in Religion and in Science." *Zygon* 20, no. 2 (1985): 125–33.

———. "Hidden Variables and the Implicate Order." *Zygon* 20, no. 2 (1985): 111–24.

———. "The Implicate Order: A New Approach to the Nature of Reality." In *Beyond Mechanism: The Universe in Recent*

Physics and Catholic Thought, edited by Davie Schindler, 13–37. Lanham, MD: University Press of America, 1986.

———. "Response to Conference Papers on 'David Bohm's Implicate Order, Physics, Philosophy, and Theology.'" *Zygon* 20, no. 2 (1985): 219–20.

———. *Wholeness and the Implicate Order*. London: Routledge, 2002.

Coakley, Sarah. *God, Sexuality, and the Self: An Essay 'On the Trinity.'* Cambridge: Cambridge University Press, 2013.

———. "Introduction: Disputed Questions in Patristic Trinitarianism." *Harvard Theological Review* 100, no. 2 (April 2007): 125–38.

Davis, Stephen, Daniel Kendall, and Gerald O'Collins, eds. *The Trinity: An Interdisciplinary Symposium on the Trinity*. Oxford: Oxford University Press, 1999.

Delio, Ilia. *Making All Things New: Catholicity, Cosmology, Consciousness*. Maryknoll, NY: Orbis Books, 2015.

———. "Theology, Metaphysics, and the Centrality of Christ." *Theological Studies* 68, no. 2 (2007): 254.

———. *The Unbearable Wholeness of Being*. Maryknoll, NY: Orbis Books, 2013.

Dunn, James D. G. *The Partings of the Ways: Between Christianity and Judaism and Their Significance for the Character of Christianity*. Philadelphia: Trinity Press International, 1991.

———. "Was Christianity a Monotheistic Faith from the Beginning?" In *The Christ and the Spirit*. Vol. 1, *Christology*, 315–44. Grand Rapids, MI: Eerdmans, 1998.

Edwards, Denis. "Athanasius' Letters to Serapion: Resource for a Twenty-First-Century Theology of God the Trinity." *Phronema* 29, no. 2 (2014): 41–64.

Fortman, Edmund J. *The Triune God: A Historical Study of the Doctrine of the Trinity*. Theological Resources. Philadelphia: Westminster, 1972.

Grenz, Stanley. *Rediscovering the Triune God: The Trinity in Contemporary Theology*. Minneapolis: Fortress Press, 2004.

Harrison, Verna E. F. "Perichoresis in the Greek Fathers." *St. Vladimir's Theological Quarterly* 35, no. 1 (1991): 53–65.

Haughey, John. *A Biography of the Spirit: There Lies the Dearest Freshness Deep Down Things*. Maryknoll, NY: Orbis Books, 2015.

Heiser, Michael S. "Monotheism, Polytheism, Monolatry, or Henotheism? Toward an Assessment of Divine Plurality in the Hebrew Bible." *Bulletin for Biblical Research* 18, no. 1 (2008): 1–30.

Horgan, John. "Quantum Philosophy." *Scientific American* 267, (1992): 94–104.

Johnson, Elizabeth. *She Who Is: The Mystery of God in Feminist Theological Discourse*. New York: Crossroad, 1992.

Jowers, Dennis W. *The Trinitarian Axiom of Karl Rahner: The Economic Trinity Is the Immanent Trinity and Vice Versa*. Lewiston, NY: Edwin Mellen Press, 2006.

Kärkkäinen, Veli-Matti. *The Trinity: Global Perspectives*. Louisville, KY: Westminster John Knox Press, 2007.

Kelly, Anthony J. *The Trinity of Love: A Theology of the Christian God*. Wilmington, DE: Michael Glazier, 1989.

Kelly, J. N. D. *Early Christian Doctrines*. Rev. ed. New York: Harper, 1978.

Kilby, Karen. "Is an Apophatic Trinitarianism Possible?" *International Journal of Systematic Theology* 12 (2010): 65–77.

———. "Perichoresis and Projection: Problems with Social Doctrines of the Trinity." *New Blackfriars* 81 (2001): 432–45.

LaCugna, Catherine Mowry. *God for Us: The Trinity and Christian Life*. San Francisco: HarperSanFrancisco, 1991.

———. "Philosophers and Theologians on the Trinity." *Modern Theology* 2, no. 3 (1986): 169–81.

———. "The Practical Trinity." *Christian Century* 109, no. 22 (2000): 15–22.

———. "The Relational God: Aquinas and Beyond." *Theological Studies* 46 (1995): 647–63.

Madden, Nicholas. "Maximus Confessor on the Holy Trinity and Deification." In *The Mystery of the Holy Trinity in the Fathers of the Church: The Proceedings of the Fourth International Patristic Conference* (Maynooth, 1999). Edited by Vincent Twomey and Lewis Ayres, 100–117. Portland, OR: Four Courts Press, 2007.

Marion, Jean-Luc. *The Erotic Phenomenon*. Translated by Stephen E. Lewis. Chicago: University of Chicago Press, 2007.

———. *God without Being: Hors-Texte*. Religion and Postmodernism. Translated by Thomas A. Carlson. Second edition. Chicago: University of Chicago Press, 2012.

———. *Prolegomena to Charity*. Translated by Stephen E. Lewis. New York: Fordham University Press, 2002.

———. "Saint Thomas d'Aquin Et l'Onto-Théologie." *Revue Thomiste* 95, no. 1 (1995): 31–66.

———. "Thomas Aquinas and Onto-Theo-Logy." In *Mystics: Presence and Aporia*, edited by Michael Kessler and Christian Sheppard, 38–74. Chicago: University of Chicago Press, 2003.

Marmion, Declan, and Rik Van Nieuwenhove. *An Introduction to the Trinity*. Introduction to Religion. Cambridge: Cambridge University Press, 2011.

Molnar, Paul. *Divine Freedom and the Doctrine of the Immanent Trinity*. New York: T & T Clark, 2002.

Moltmann, Jürgen. *Sun of Righteousness, Arise!: God's Future for Humanity and the Earth*. Translated by Margaret Kohl. Minneapolis: Fortress Press, 2010.

O'Collins, Gerald. *The Tripersonal God: Understanding and Interpreting the Trinity*. New York: Paulist Press, 1999.

Otto, Randall. "The Use and Abuse of Perichoresis in Recent Theology." *Scottish Journal of Theology* 54 (2001): 366–84.

Peìrez, Aìngel Cordovilla. "The Trinitarian Concept of Person." In *Rethinking Trinitarian Theology: Disputed Questions and Contemporary Issues in Trinitarian Theology*, edited by Giulio Maspero and Robert J. Wozniak, 105–45. London: T & T Clark, 2012.

Peters, Ted. "David Bohm, Postmodernism, and the Divine." *Zygon* 20, no. 2 (1985): 193–217.

———. *God as Trinity: Relationality and Temporality in Divine Life*. Louisville, KY: Westminster/John Knox Press, 1993.

Rahner, Karl. "Christian Dying." In *God and Revelation,* vol. 18 in *Theological Investigations.* Translated by Edward Quinn, 226–56. New York: Crossroad, 1983.

———. "Current Problems in Christology." In *God, Christ, Mary, and Grace*, vol. 1 in *Theological Investigations.* Translated by Cornelius Ernst, 149–200. Baltimore: Helicon Press, 1961.

———. *Foundations of Christian Faith: An Introduction to the Idea of Christianity*. Translated by William Dych. New York: Crossroad, 1978.

———. "Jesus Christ." *Habitus to Materialism,* vol. 3 in *Sacramentum Mundi: An Encyclopedia of Theology*, 192–209. New York: Herder and Herder, 1969.

———. "On the Theology of the Incarnation." In *More Recent Writings,* vol. 4 in *Theological Investigations.* Translated by Kevin Smyth, 105–20. Baltimore: Helicon Press, 1966.

———. "The Position of Christology in the Church between Exegesis and Dogmatics." In *Confrontations I,* vol. 11 in *Theological Investigations*. Translated by David Bourke, 185–214. New York: Seabury, 1974.

———. "The Theology of the Symbol." In *More Recent Writings,* vol. 4 in *Theological Investigations.* Translated by Kevin Smyth, 221–52. Baltimore: Helicon Press, 1961.

———. *The Trinity*. Translated by Joseph Donceel. New York: Crossroad, 1997.

Rauser, Randal. "Rahner's Rule: An Emperor without Clothes?" *International Journal of Systematic Theology* 7, no. 1 (2005): 81–94.

Russell, Heidi. "Efficacious and Sufficient Grace: God's One Offer of Self-Communication as Accepted or Rejected." *Philosophy and Theology* 22, no. 1–2 (2010): 353–72.

———. *The Heart of Rahner: The Theological Implications of Andrew Tallon's Theory of Triune Consciousness*. Marquette Studies in Theology 64. Milwaukee: Marquette University Press, 2009.

———. "Quantum Anthropology: Reimaging the Human Person as Body/Spirit." *Theological Studies* 74, no. 4 (December 2013): 934–59.

———. *Quantum Shift: Theological and Pastoral Implications of Contemporary Developments in Science*. Collegeville, MN: Liturgical Press, 2015.

Russell, Robert John. "The Physics of David Bohm and Its Relevance to Philosophy and Theology." *Zygon* 20, no. 2 (1985): 135–58.

Schmitt, John. "Israel as the Son of God in Torah." *Biblical Theology Bulletin* 34 (2004): 69–79.

Sharpe, Kevin J. "Holomovement Metaphysics and Theology." *Zygon* 28, no. 1 (1993): 47–60.

Smith, Mark S. *The Memoirs of God: History, Memory, and the Experience of the Divine in Ancient Israel*. Minneapolis: Fortress Press, 2004.

Smolin, Lee. *Three Roads to Quantum Gravity*. New York: Basic Books, 2001.

———. *Time Reborn: From the Crisis in Physics to the Future of the Universe*. Boston: Houghton Mifflin Harcourt, 2013.

Soulen, R. Kendall. *The Divine Name(s) and the Holy Trinity,* vol. 1, *Distinguishing the Voices*. Louisville, KY: Westminster John Knox Press, 2011.

Tanner, Kathryn. "Social Trinitarianism and Its Critics." In *Rethinking Trinitarian Theology: Disputed Questions and Contemporary Issues in Trinitarian Theology*, edited by Giulio Maspero and Robert J. Wozniak, 368–86. London: T & T Clark, 2012.

Tollefsen, Torstein. "Christocentric Cosmology." In *The Oxford Handbook of Maximus the Confessor*, edited by Pauline Allen and Bronwen Neil, 307–21. Oxford: Oxford University Press, 2015.

———. *The Christocentric Cosmology of St. Maximus the Confessor*. Oxford: Oxford University Press, 2008.

Woloschak, Gayle E. "The Broad Science-Religion Dialogue: Maximus, Augustine, and Others." In *Science and the Eastern Orthodox Church*, edited by Daniel Buxhoeveden and Gale Woloschak, 133–40. Farnham, Surrey, England: Ashgate, 2011.

Zizioulas, Jean Metr. "The Doctrine of the Holy Trinity: The Significance of the Cappadocian Contribution." In *Trinitarian Theology Today: Essays on Divine Being and Act*, edited by Christoph Schwöbel, 44–60. Edinburgh: T & T Clark, 1995.

Index